IMPROVING TREATMENT COMPLIANCE

Counseling and Systems Strategies for Substance Abuse and Dual Disorders

Dennis C. Daley
Allan Zuckoff

HAZELDEN®

Hazelden
Center City, Minnesota 55012-0176
1-800-328-0094
1-651-257-1331 (Fax)
www.hazelden.org

Library of Congress Cataloging-in-Publication Data
Daley, Dennis C.
Improving treatment compliance : counseling and systems strategies for substance abuse and dual disorders / Dennis C. Daley, Allan Zuckoff.
p. cm.
Includes bibliographical references and index.
ISBN: 1-56838-281-2
1. Substance abuse—Treatment. 2. Dual diagnosis—Treatment. 3. Patient compliance. 4. Addicts—Counseling of. I. Zuckoff, Allan 1960- . II. Title.
RC564.D345 1999
616.86'06—dc21 98-47969
CIP

Editor's note

All the stories in this book are based on actual experiences. The names and details have been changed to protect the privacy of the people involved.

03 02 5
Cover design by David Spohn
Interior design by Donna Burch
Typesetting by Stanton Publication Services, Inc.

For Bonnie, who has taught me most about empathy,
and Alexander, who shows me its power.
AZ

To my son, Chris, who continues to bring
tremendous joy to my life. It is a pleasure to watch
you develop into such a fine young man.
DD

Contents

Charts

Acknowledgments

We wish to thank the following individuals for their help and support in the preparation of this book: Ihsan Salloum, M.D., M.P.H.; Crystal Spotts, M.Ed.; and our colleagues at the Center for Psychiatric and Chemical Dependency Services for their involvement in clinical protocols aimed at improving compliance among our clinic clients; Michael Thase, M.D., for his support of our clinical work and research on compliance and motivation at Western Psychiatric Institute and Clinic; Karen Chernyaev of Hazelden for her excellent editorial support and interest in making this project feasible; Judy Peacock and Kathryn Kjorlien for their outstanding copyedit of the book; Cindy Hurney for her outstanding help in library research, word processing, organizing and formatting the book, and generally keeping us on track when we threatened to go astray; and Natalie Daley, M.S.W., for her critical review of the book. We also are grateful to the National Institute on Drug Abuse for support of our research on developing clinical interventions to improve motivation for change and compliance with treatment. —DD

My gratitude begins with my mother, Gerry, whose sensitivity to others gave me whatever quantity of that trait I possess; my father, Sid, my first teacher, whose passion for ideas is the source of my own; and my brother, Mitchell, with whom I've shared a bond that has been tested and found true. I am also deeply grateful to M.C. Dillon and members of the philosophy department at SUNY–Binghamton, and to the late Charles Maes and members of the department of psychology at Duquesne University, for all they taught me. My co-author, Dennis Daley, has provided me with opportunity and encouragement far beyond what I could have imagined when he took a chance on me five years ago. My clients, who must of course remain anonymous here, are nonetheless present in every word, much to this book's enrichment and my own. And most especially, I am grateful to my family: my loving wife, Bonnie Gorscak, Ph.D., my most important teacher in the area of clinical skill; and my son, Alexander, my favorite and my best.—AZ

For information about workshops on Compliance Enhancement Strategies, Motivational Therapy, or other topics related to recovery from addiction or dual disorders, call 1-412-383-2700, e-mail daleydc@msx.upmc.edu or zuckoffam@msx.upmc.edu, or write to the authors at W.P.I.C., 3811 O'Hara Street, Pittsburgh, Pennsylvania 15213.

PART one

Overview of Compliance Problems, Causes, and Effects

Chapter 1

Introduction and Overview

Introduction

Substance use disorders are very common in the United States. More than 16 percent of adults meet the American Psychiatric Association (APA) criteria for alcohol, drug, or multiple substance abuse or dependency at some point in their lives. Many of these individuals also have dual disorders—a psychiatric disorder as well as a substance use disorder. Almost four in ten people with an alcohol use disorder and over five in ten of those with a drug use disorder also meet the APA criteria for a psychiatric disorder at some point in their lives.[1] Individuals with substance use or dual disorders are commonly found in drug and alcohol and mental health treatment programs, in medical delivery systems, in criminal justice systems, in homeless and housing programs, and in other social service agencies.

Individuals who have multiple psychosocial problems and need treatment as well as other social services frequently have difficulty complying with treatment. Poor compliance is a serious problem evident at all levels of care for substance abuse and dual disorders (coexisting psychiatric disorders) including inpatient, community residential, partial hospital, intensive outpatient, outpatient, and aftercare programs. These individuals may fail to enter treatment and to follow through with the initial evaluation. Or, they frequently drop out of treatment prematurely. Poor retention, or failure to remain in substance abuse treatment, is associated with poor outcomes; many studies show that longer treatment improves outcomes.[2]

Clients who comply with treatment and stay in for an adequate amount of time do much better than dropouts. A recent report on treatment effectiveness issued by the National Institute on Drug Abuse (NIDA) states that "retention has been our most powerful and consistent predictor of treatment outcomes."[3] Clearly, better treatment compliance and retention lead to more positive clinical outcomes in relation to alcohol or drug dependency, psychiatric symptoms, and psychosocial functioning (including decreased criminal behavior). Substance abuse treatments are considered effective to the extent that they demonstrate the ability to retain patients.[4]

We became interested in this important clinical area of client compliance out of necessity. In our treatment clinic, as well as many other treatment clinics for substance abuse or dual disorders, we found that poor compliance was common and a source of frustration for clinicians. In presenting lectures and workshops within our medical center and throughout the United States and Europe, we found considerable interest in the problem among professionals from all backgrounds and disciplines. Addictions professionals expressed concern over the high rates of poor compliance and the impact of poor compliance on sobriety rates. They asked about the causes of compliance problems and ways to motivate clients to follow through with their treatment plan or move from one level of care to another. Psychiatrists, psychologists, social workers, nurses, and other professionals involved in taking care of clients with dual disorders noted that poor compliance with therapy or psychiatric medications almost invariably leads to a worsening of symptoms and rehospitalization, especially for more chronically impaired clients.

As we changed the ways in which we thought about compliance and in how we delivered clinical services in our inpatient and outpatient programs, we were able to make a difference in the compliance rates of clients with substance abuse or dual disorders. We also were able to influence counselors to change their behavior, which, in turn, increased client willingness to keep scheduled counseling appointments. The noticeable results improved treatment outcome and the morale of counseling staff.

Our goal in writing this book is to help clinicians and treatment agencies better understand and address the problem of poor compliance among clients who have substance abuse disorders, including those with dual disorders. We will review a continuum of compliance; identify ways in which poor compliance manifests itself; discuss effects of poor compliance on the client, family, and professional caregiver; and identify multiple factors contributing to compliance problems. The major thrust of the book will be on discussing a variety of practical clinical strategies and treatment system interventions that can help improve compliance among clients with substance abuse or dual disorders. We will give considerable attention to interventions counselors can use to motivate clients—from the initial telephone call through aftercare counseling.

The strategies presented in this book are based on our extensive clinical experience addressing compliance issues, on quality assurance and quality improvement studies conducted in our treatment programs, and on our involvement in federally funded research grants.[5] We also integrate information from empirical studies and clinical reports on compliance-related issues across a wide range of problems including substance abuse, psychiatric illness, dual disorders, family problems, and medical disorders. Rather than provide statistics and details from the literature, we focus on the major findings. Readers can consult the extensive notes section for more information on any of the issues discussed in this book.

Poor compliance is one of the most significant barriers to providing effective treatment to individuals with substance abuse or dual disorders; we strongly believe that this practical counseling manual will enable clinicians to more effectively address this problem in their day-to-day work with clients. We also believe that treatment clinics and programs can improve their overall rates of compliance by changing how services are delivered or monitored.

Definitions and Continuum of Compliance

Compliance and *adherence* are often used interchangeably in the literature, although some authors refer to adherence as being more active and voluntary than compliance, which is viewed as being more passive. In this book, we define "compliance" as the extent to which the patient or client follows the agreed-on treatment plan. Compliance covers a variety of behaviors such as

- entering into a treatment agreement
- continuing the treatment agreement
- keeping scheduled appointments
- following medication regimens in cases in which medicines are used to treat the substance use disorder, mental health disorder, or both disorders
- making lifestyle changes worked out with the counselor (e.g., avoiding or minimizing contact with high-

risk people, places, events, and things; modifying diet; following an exercise program; attending self-help meetings)

As with other processes, compliance is not an all-or-none phenomenon. Clients are seldom either compliant or noncompliant. Rather, as shown in chart 1, they can be assessed on a continuum from total compliance to total noncompliance.

Chart 1 Continuum of Compliance				
Totally Compliant	Mostly Compliant	Partially Compliant	Minimally Compliant	Noncompliant

The following case examples illustrate different levels of compliance among clients in treatment for substance abuse or dual disorders. These examples also illustrate consequences associated with varying levels of compliance.

- *Totally Compliant*
  Bill, a high school teacher recovering from alcoholism, has only changed one scheduled counseling appointment and regularly attends two AA meetings each week. When he travels out of town, he still attends AA meetings. Bill always follows through and completes assigned therapeutic readings or agreed-on recovery tasks. Overall, his compliance is outstanding and he feels that this has had a positive impact on his ability to remain sober for over one year. Bill reports that attending AA meetings regularly helps him during the occasional periods when his motivation wavers a bit. He's discovered that by sticking with the meetings, even when he feels indifferent, he's able to work through periods of self-doubt and to deal with thoughts of drinking alcohol. Bill's job is no longer in jeopardy and his marriage

is now stable. During his first attempt at recovery, when Bill's compliance was rather poor, he faced the possibility of losing his marriage and his job. Clearly, improved compliance has led to many positive benefits for him.

- *Mostly Compliant*
  Nancy, a nurse recovering from alcoholism, drug dependency, and depression, has kept about 80 percent of her scheduled therapy appointments. While she generally takes her antidepressants as prescribed, on two occasions she was late in filling her prescriptions and missed over a week's worth of medicine each time. She also reports being somewhat erratic in attending self-help groups and following through with therapeutic assignments. Overall, she's doing fairly well, although at times she experiences brief bouts of depression and problems coping with her teenage children. Nancy reports that when she misses her aftercare group, she's more likely to experience strong desires to use drugs and feels more negative about her recovery.

- *Minimally Compliant*
  Ken suffers from schizophrenia, depression, alcoholism, and marijuana dependency. He has been hospitalized more than ten times following episodes of psychotic deterioration and symptoms of severe depression. After being discharged from the hospital, he has either failed to show up for the partial hospital or outpatient program or dropped out after only a few weeks in treatment. Ken would also frequently stop taking antipsychotic medications and resume marijuana use, which often led to rehospitalization. On several occasions he's been kicked out of long-term community residential treatment programs because of his failure to attend a partial hospital program and his persistent abuse of alcohol and marijuana.

Chapter 2

Types of Compliance Problems

Introduction

This chapter focuses on the various ways in which poor compliance surfaces among clients with substance abuse or dual disorders (see chart 3, page 19). We begin by discussing compliance problems related to entering treatment or to the early phase of treatment. We then address compliance problems with ongoing attendance at treatment sessions or self-help programs, with medications, and with the completion of therapeutic assignments or goals. Finally, we discuss various ways to measure compliance in clinical care.

Treatment Entry

Many potential clients who make an initial appointment for an evaluation for treatment fail to show up for it. Several studies have found that the majority of substance abuse clients fail to follow through with their initial appointment.[1] In our first study of dual diagnosis clients who were referred to our clinic, more than 60 percent failed to attend the initial evaluation required to enter outpatient treatment.[2]

The same holds true for individuals who complete psychiatric care in an acute care hospital program, a short-term inpatient addiction program, or a longer-term residential treatment program for addiction.[3] Many fail to successfully make the transition to a partial hospital program, an intensive outpatient program, or an outpatient or aftercare program. Individuals in need of hospitalization or residential treatment typically have substance abuse or dual disorders of such severity that ongoing follow-up care is needed after initial stabilization, yet many fail to enter a subsequent level of care.

Early Attrition from Treatment

Studies of substance abusers consistently show that most attrition, or falling away, occurs early in the treatment process with the greatest majority of clients dropping out within the first month of treatment.[4] In our work, we, too, have found the first month of outpatient treatment to be the highest risk period for early attrition among dual diagnosis clients. Compared with clients who do not drop out early from treatment, those who drop out during the first month are less likely to show improvement in their psychiatric symptoms, more likely to resume substance abuse, and more likely to be rehospitalized in a psychiatric hospital as a result of significant worsening of their symptoms.[5]

The following clinical examples illustrate the difficulties in getting clients into outpatient treatment.

- Ron, age thirty-two and single, works in his father's business. Following detoxification for heroin addiction at a local hospital, Ron was referred for outpatient care. He showed up two hours late for his initial evaluation and was rescheduled for the next day. He then failed to show up for this appointment. The counselor telephoned Ron to try to ascertain his current clinical status and treatment needs. Ron did not return the counselor's telephone calls, nor did he respond to a letter sent to his home requesting that he call to reschedule an appointment.

- Wanda, twenty-six years old and the mother of two children, was diagnosed with cocaine dependence, alcohol abuse, recurrent major depression, and a mixed personality disorder. Her inpatient treatment team referred her to outpatient treatment. Wanda failed to show up for her initial appointment. Because she did not have a telephone, the clinic sent her a letter, offering her another appointment. She finally entered outpatient treatment a month after receiving this letter.

Treatment Session Attendance

Compliance problems frequently show in clients missing their scheduled individual, family, group, or medication sessions with addiction or mental health professionals. While some clients miss the majority of their sessions, others are erratic and inconsistent in their attendance. In our experience, compliance tends to be worse with group treatment sessions compared with individual sessions. Despite the various reasons clients provide for missing treatment appointments, we believe that missed sessions tend to reflect problems in the client-therapist relationship, problems with the client's motivation to change, practical problems such as lack of transportation, or problems due to high levels of social anxiety and related avoidant behavior.

Poor compliance also shows in tardiness. Clients may show up significantly late for a session, leaving insufficient time to focus on problems and therapeutic goals. While there are occasional legitimate reasons for lateness, such as an unexpected or uncontrollable problem with transportation, we believe that in most instances lateness reflects the client's ambivalence about treatment and change, a problem with self-disclosure, a problem in the therapeutic relationship, a problem with a current relapse, or a self-sabotaging pattern of behavior. In the last case, the behavior permeates other areas of the client's life as well.

Many clients who drop out early do not receive an adequate "dose" of treatment and do not benefit from what little treatment they do receive. While early treatment dropout occurs in all treatment settings among all types of substance abuse and dual disorders, it appears that clients with cocaine problems and those with addiction combined with a personality disorder are at greatest risk for poor compliance and early treatment dropout.[6]

Therapeutic Goals

When entering treatment, clients agree on individualized goals related to their substance abuse, psychiatric illness, or other related areas of their lives. When substance abuse is involved as a major problem, clients may verbally agree on the goal of abstinence from alcohol or other drugs. Yet they fail to comply with this goal because they haven't accepted it as *their* goal; they have no intention of working toward abstinence, or they struggle with achieving abstinence. Abstinence is considered the appropriate goal in cases of dependency since continued use puts the client at risk for a variety of problems. However, it may take the counselor some time to get the client to accept and comply with the goal of abstinence.

While some clients remain abstinent from all substances,

others comply with the goal of abstinence from the primary substance of use but continue to abuse other types of substances. For example, many cocaine addicts continue to abuse alcohol or marijuana while agreeing to abstain from cocaine. They tend to see other substances as much less harmful than their drug of choice.

Therapeutic Assignments

Clinicians frequently prescribe or help clients develop therapeutic assignments to work on between scheduled treatment sessions. These recovery-oriented assignments provide clients the opportunity to educate themselves in the area of concern, to increase self-awareness, and to practice or implement cognitive, behavioral, or interpersonal change strategies. Some common recovery-related assignments include

- reading materials on recovery from addiction, mental health disorders, or dual disorders
- keeping written records of any substance use, cravings, or close calls as well as the context in which these occur
- maintaining journals or logs in which moods or feelings (e.g., anger, anxiety, depression, boredom) are monitored
- maintaining journals or logs in which specific thoughts, cognitive distortions, and counter strategies are monitored and recorded
- maintaining journals or logs of persistent symptoms of psychiatric illness (e.g., chronic depressed feelings, hallucinations, delusions)
- completing a daily or weekly inventory

- practicing interpersonal behavior such as assertiveness by saying no to a specific request, by expressing feelings, or by making a request of another person
- developing an activities schedule to structure the day and to find time for self-care and for recreation
- participating in "working" a Twelve Step program
- seeking out a sponsor in a Twelve Step program
- attending an agreed-on number of self-help meetings

Compliance problems show in the client's failure to complete part or all of the therapeutic assignment or in a hasty, half-hearted attempt to complete it. The client may proclaim "I forgot, I was too busy, I didn't have time" or give some other rationalization for failure to comply, even if he or she agreed to complete the task prior to the end of the previous treatment session.

The following clinical example illustrates a problem following through with a therapeutic assignment.

- Liz, age thirty-nine, is a divorced mother of three children. She has been in treatment for recurrent major depression, generalized anxiety disorder, alcohol dependence, and benzodiazepine abuse. Two of her goals were to decrease boredom and to increase her social interaction so that she could make at least one new friend in recovery. Liz agreed to go to a local recovery club once a week and to socialize after AA meetings. She also agreed to make a list of social and recreational activities that she had enjoyed prior to the onset of her addiction. This list was to be used as a basis for developing a weekly schedule of social and recreational activities. However, Liz attended the recovery club on only one occasion and did not complete her written list of social and recreational activities.

Self-Help Program Participation

Self-help programs play a major role in recovery from substance abuse or dual disorders. Clients with previous self-help program involvement often report specific ways in which these programs aided their recovery, including learning how to cope with desires to use substances, learning how to reach out for help and support from other members, and learning ways to change negative thinking associated with relapse. Yet poor compliance with self-help programs is common. Some clients don't give the program a fair chance. They attend only a single session and then claim that they get nothing from the meetings or that self-help programs can't help them. Others attend meetings erratically and don't develop the discipline or commitment needed to participate in meetings regularly. Clients also fail to follow through with agreements to seek and to rely on sponsors in these programs.

Medication

Noncompliance with medications prescribed to treat addiction (e.g., Antabuse or ReVia for alcohol problems; Trexan for opiate dependence) or to treat a concurrent psychiatric illness is a common and serious problem that has major implications for relapse and rehospitalization.[7] These compliance problems show in failing to take medications as prescribed (e.g., not taking enough medication, skipping doses, or taking too much medication), stopping medications without first consulting the prescribing physician or a counselor, running out of medications and failing to get prescriptions renewed, mixing medications with alcohol or other drugs, or taking a temporary "medication holiday" in order to get high on alcohol or other drugs.

The following clinical examples show the consequences of noncompliance with medications.

- Matt, a thirty-nine-year-old married father of one, recently lost his job as a result of behaviors associated with alcoholism. He was diagnosed with alcohol dependence and depression, but initially refused AA, outpatient groups, and an intensive outpatient program. Matt stated he didn't think his "alcohol problem" warranted abstinence. However, after reluctantly attending several outpatient sessions, he changed his mind and agreed to try to abstain from alcohol. Matt requested Antabuse based on his having used this medication several years prior to the current treatment episode. For several months, he managed to abstain from alcohol and took the Antabuse as prescribed. Then, Matt "forgot" to get his prescription renewed and ran out of Antabuse. Within three weeks, he relapsed to alcohol use.
- Larry—twenty-five years old, single, and unemployed—has a history of chronic mental illness and substance abuse. He was diagnosed as having schizophrenia, a mood disorder, and alcohol and marijuana dependence. His doctor prescribed an antipsychotic, a mood stabilizer, and an antidepressant. Larry's medication compliance varied from excellent to poor. During times in which Larry took his medications as prescribed, his chronic mental symptoms were fairly well controlled. Although he still experienced some persistent mood and psychotic symptoms, they were much improved and had little adverse effect on his functioning. However, when Larry's medication compliance was poor, his psychiatric symptoms worsened and his risk of psychiatric rehospitalization increased.

Ways to Measure Compliance

Compliance can be measured in a variety of ways. The clinician can ask the client or significant other (e.g., family member) direct questions regarding abstinence, attendance at self-help meetings, medication use, or recovery-oriented therapeutic assignments. Recovery assignments can be reviewed in sessions to determine if the client has been completing them. Urinalysis or breathalyzer tests can be administered to detect alcohol or other drug use. Blood tests often help determine if a therapeutic dose of certain types of medications, such as those used to treat mood disorders, is in the client's bloodstream.

The following clinical example illustrates how a blood test revealed medication noncompliance.

- Kate initially reported that she was taking lithium as prescribed. When her psychiatrist ordered a lithium blood level and the results showed a low level of the medication in her blood, she reluctantly admitted that she had been only about 60 percent compliant with the medication. This finding led to a thorough discussion of her concerns and negative feelings about medications and an analysis of benefits versus negative effects.

Some clients will initially passively accept medication recommendations only to later show their resistance through poor compliance with the medication regime.

Treatment programs or clinics can measure compliance by monitoring the percentage of sessions attended by each client. This can be done for each clinician as well as for the entire treatment program. Compliance can also be monitored by examining completion rates of treatment at various

Chart 2 Sample Clinician Compliance		
Clinician	Client Compliance Rate with Scheduled Individual Sessions in an Outpatient Drug, Alcohol, and Dual Diagnosis Clinic	70% +/- Threshold
1	48%	-22%
2	67%	-3%
3	70%	-
4	72%	+2%
5	76%	+6%

stages. For example, an outpatient program can document the percentage of clients who comply with their initial evaluation, complete the early phase of treatment (e.g., one month), and complete a certain course of treatment, which can be defined as a specific number of sessions, a specific length of time in treatment, or both. Inpatient, or residential, rehabilitation programs can monitor compliance by examining completion rates, early dropout rates, and follow-through with the initial aftercare sessions. Clients may leave inpatient residential programs against the advice of treatment staff or due to major violations of program rules, leading to an administrative discharge. Actual rates of dropout can then be compared with a threshold identified as acceptable for a particular program.

Chart 2 shows the client compliance rate for five counselors in an outpatient program. As indicated, the five counselors varied in their ability to meet the required threshold of 70 percent compliance with individual scheduled appointments. Three exceeded or met the threshold and two were below. However, one counselor was 22 percent below the accepted threshold. This alerts the supervisor that some intervention is needed to help the counselor improve client compliance with scheduled individual appointments. If cases

Chart 3 Ways Poor Compliance Shows
• Delay in Entering Treatment • Failure to Enter Treatment • Missing Treatment Sessions • Lateness for Treatment Sessions • Failure to Work on Treatment Goals • Failure to Work on or Complete Therapeutic Assignments • Dropping Out of Treatment before Completion • Missing Self-Help Meetings • Failure to Take Medications as Prescribed • Stopping Medications Prematurely

are generally distributed randomly to all counseling staff, the supervisor could assume that compliance rates should be fairly equal. Major deviations from the average or acceptable compliance rates can be dealt with on an individual basis.

Chapter 3

Factors Affecting Client Compliance

Introduction

Many factors impact compliance problems and early termination from treatment (see chart 4, page 40). Usually a combination of factors, rather than one in particular, contributes to poor compliance. These factors include client characteristics, symptoms of illness, interpersonal or relationship variables, and treatment- and system-related variables.[1] This chapter discusses each category of variables that contributes to compliance problems.

Client Variables

Many client-related internal and external factors impact compliance. These include motivation to change; beliefs about a problem and what is needed to change it; stigma associated with having a problem, disorder, or illness; expectations of treatment; satisfaction with counselor or therapy; personality; and life events or problems that occur during the course of treatment.

Motivation

Many people with alcohol or other drug use disorders enter treatment primarily to address problems caused by substance use rather than to reduce substance use.[2] For example, a client may initially seek treatment to comply with a court mandate, to save a job, to save a marriage, or to avoid some potential negative consequence if treatment is not sought. The client with little or no motivation to reduce substance use is less likely to keep treatment appointments, to take medications as prescribed, or to attend self-help program meetings. Motivation is often low or externally based in the early phase of treatment. If there are no external factors pressuring clients to participate in treatment or monitoring treatment attendance, they are less likely to be compliant. The client's ambivalence and disinterest in complying with treatment will change when motivation increases.

In our experience, ambivalence and low motivation are among the most common reasons clients fail to attend outpatient or aftercare sessions following inpatient or residential treatment for addiction or dual disorders. A young woman with cocaine dependency and alcoholism put this in perspective when she said to her counselor: *When I really want help and feel I need it, I go to sessions and do what I'm supposed to. This really helps me stay sober and clean. The problem I have is when I don't give a damn about my recovery. That's when I blow off sessions. It's like why even bother going through with it if I don't want it. My motivation changes day-to-day.*

Beliefs

The client's beliefs about the substance use or psychiatric disorder and the treatment of these disorders affect motivation and subsequently compliance. Clients who deny and fail to accept their problem believe that their substance use is under control or that treatment isn't necessary. They will be less motivated to change and comply with treatment than clients who accept their problem and believe that they need help.

The client who believes that alcohol or drug dependency is a disease, or that psychiatric illness is primarily biological in nature, may take a passive approach to participating in treatment. This client may not appreciate or value the importance of therapy, the importance of personal involvement in a plan of recovery, or the importance of making specific changes to cope with these disorders. Instead, the client may rely on the professionals to "provide treatment" and develop unrealistic expectations about counseling or the role of medications in treatment. We have seen clients with dual disorders, for example, who believed that their psychiatric symptoms could only be changed by an increase in the dose of medications or a new type of medication. These clients did not value individual or group therapy. As a result, they refused or missed group treatments, even if group was highly recommended by the treatment team.

Stigma

The client who feels stigmatized for having an alcohol or other drug problem or dual disorder may resist treatment. Guilt, shame, or embarrassment can make it difficult to accept help from others. For some clients, having a drug or alcohol problem or being dual disordered is quite demoralizing. As one client put it: *When I first came to grips that I was a drug addict, I was devastated. It was so hard to accept the need for help. When I first got off drugs, the idea of being a recovering drug addict bothered me.*

Expectations

Clients have expectations of treatment, regardless of their motivation to change. The client who expects treatment to fail or be ineffective is more likely to give up and not comply with treatment. On the other hand, if clients have high expectations of treatment and their expectations aren't met, they are at risk for reduced treatment compliance. For example, Rose, a woman with a long history of severe alcoholism and multiple relapses, attended a new treatment program that emphasized relapse prevention. She expected that this new "program"—rather than her *application* of the information and skills taught to her in this program—would make her recovery more successful than in the past. When Rose discovered that recovery still required diligence, consistency, discipline, and hard work, and that she still would experience irrational desires or strong cravings to drink, she felt disappointed and let down. Not long after, she became erratic in attending aftercare counseling and AA meetings and subsequently relapsed once again. A very common phenomenon is the client who gives up too quickly when expectations aren't met or rough spots appear in the recovery journey.

Satisfaction with Treatment

Clients' overall satisfaction with the treatment process and their relationships with the counselor or other members of the treatment team impact compliance. If clients feel dissatisfied and that the treatment is not helping, they are not likely to continue to follow the treatment plan and attend sessions. Similarly, if clients feel dissatisfied with their experience in a self-help program, they are at risk to cut down or stop participation.

Personality

Personality traits have a large impact on behaviors and treatment compliance. Impulsive clients often miss sessions or drop out prematurely because they are unable to make a commitment, cannot discipline themselves to keep regular appointments, and become easily frustrated if they feel counseling sessions or self-help meetings are not giving them what they want. Clients who are passive, apathetic, indifferent, or anti-authority often evidence poor compliance. One client, known for his frequent conflicts with mental health professionals, put it this way: *I knew my counselor was trying to help me when he leaned on me to go to NA (Narcotics Anonymous) meetings and told me to cut loose some of my friends, guys I'd been getting high with. I mean I was messing up big time and needed help real bad to get my life together. If this wasn't bad enough, I got a sponsor who also told me how I could stay clean. I just didn't like the idea of being told what to do. So what did I do? I dropped my sponsor and my counselor. You see what it got me, back to where I was before.*

Other Addictions, Life Events, or Problems

Other addictions, practical problems, and life issues affect compliance. These can include compulsive gambling or sexual behavior, medical or physical problems, difficulty with child care, illness of a child or family member, lack of transportation to treatment sessions or self-help programs, incarceration, lack of time, and limited financial resources to pay for professional treatments such as medications or therapy sessions. A single mother with a limited income may miss counseling sessions because she cannot afford to pay a babysitter and has limited access to free baby-sitting from family, friends, or neighbors. Once she starts missing sessions and loses continuity of care, she's more likely to drop out of treatment completely. We take care of many clients from low socioeconomic backgrounds in our treatment clinic. While we've had cases in which mothers brought their babies or young children on public transportation to our clinic because they did not want to miss their appointments, more often than not, mothers miss sessions when child care cannot be arranged. Unexpected life events (loss of a job, relationship, or financial security) may occur during the course of treatment. Any number of events can cause a serious crisis for the client and result in reduced compliance.

Illness and Symptom-Related Variables

Compliance is affected by numerous factors associated with having an alcohol, drug, and/or psychiatric problem. Specific symptoms of a disorder, anxiety experienced in relation to social interaction, strong obsessions or cravings for alcohol or other drugs, as well as actual improvement in symptoms or problems for which a client originally sought help may affect a client's desire or ability to comply with a treatment plan.

Symptoms of Addiction and/or Psychiatric Illness

Impaired judgment is associated with the active phase of addiction as well as with psychiatric disorders such as bipolar illness, personality disorders, and schizophrenia. Impaired judgment shows in many different ways, including poor compliance with treatment. Lethargy, poor concentration, confusion, and low motivation are common symptoms of depression and schizophrenia and affect treatment compliance. Clients with long-term, chronic, and persistent forms of mental illness may feel hopeless or experience persistent symptoms such as hallucinations, delusions, severe anxiety, or severe mood disturbances. These mental states interfere with decision making in regard to treatment compliance.

Social Anxiety

Social anxiety and avoidant behaviors are very common among clients with substance abuse or dual disorders.

Clients who feel nervous and uncomfortable in groups of people will be reluctant to attend group treatment sessions or self-help meetings and miss sessions or fail to attend altogether. They may not even be aware of the degree to which their social anxiety affects attendance. The professional counselor or therapist also may not be aware of this anxiety and its impact on the client's willingness to participate. One client, whose counselor routinely instructed him to attend several AA meetings each week, reported the following about his experience in AA: *I knew AA could help me stay sober because of what other alcoholics told me. But I had trouble talking in front of people and was terrified of discussion meetings. So I tried a few lead meetings. When I was asked by the chair of one meeting if I would read the Twelve Traditions, I became overwhelmed with fear and nervousness. I couldn't do it. It was so embarrassing and uncomfortable I quit going to meetings altogether.* Because the counselor never addressed the client's anxiety and the client did not discuss it in counseling, the client was put in a situation in which he was likely to fail.

Obsessions or Cravings to Use Substances

Clients working toward initiating sobriety or those in the early phases of sobriety often experience strong obsessions or cravings to use alcohol or other drugs. Some experience acute or protracted physical withdrawal symptoms that compel them to use substances and not comply with treatment. Clients without strategies to manage obsessions or cravings are at risk to use substances. Once they lapse or relapse, they may then become noncompliant with treatment sessions or self-help meetings.

Previous History of Illness and Relapse

Clients with a history of poor treatment compliance—for example, leaving hospital or residential treatment programs against medical advice, dropping out of partial hospital, outpatient, or aftercare programs, erratic attendance at scheduled treatment sessions or self-help meetings, or failure to take medications as prescribed—are at high risk for continued poor compliance, unless their attitude and motivation have changed markedly.[3] Although any client can change his or her pattern of compliance, a previous history of poor compliance is a major risk factor and should alert the counselor that this is potentially a high-risk client. For example, Roger has had over twenty admissions to detoxification, rehabilitation, and psychiatric dual diagnosis programs but has followed through with aftercare treatment on only two occasions. Roger's chronic and persistent noncompliance has played a major role in his frequent return to expensive, inpatient treatment. The counselor who encounters Roger in any treatment setting would be wise to anticipate noncompliance and address this in therapy sessions to increase the likelihood that Roger will follow up with aftercare.

Failure to Catch Early Warning Signs of Relapse

Warning signs frequently precede relapse to substance use or psychiatric disorders. Clients who spot these early and take action are more likely to remain in treatment and comply with their plan than those who fail to identify these early signs and take action. One woman stated: *I knew when I felt suicidal I should tell someone and do something, but I thought maybe these feelings would just go away. Instead, they got worse. Feeling desperate, I smoked crack and relapsed after being clean for over a year. The thing is, I knew I was headed back to crack if I didn't do the things I learned in treatment, but I just ignored all the signs instead.* This woman's experience is not all that uncommon. Many clients do not take action when early indicators of relapse are present.

Improvement in Symptoms or Problems

While client- and illness-related variables can lead to poor compliance or early termination from professional treatment, clients may also stop treatment because they are doing better. Clients with substance use disorders may stop or significantly reduce alcohol or other drug use and feel treatment is no longer needed as they have their problems under control. Or, they may experience improvement in the related life problems that led them to treatment in the first place, which, in turn, leads them to believe treatment is no longer needed. Dual-disordered clients with additional psychiatric disorders may similarly experience improvement in specific symptoms or functioning and no longer feel treatment is needed. In other cases, clients may believe that their needs are being adequately met by self-help programs and hence drop out early from treatment. Unfortunately, not all clients discuss their desire to terminate treatment as a result of improvements; some simply stop attending sessions. Therefore, counselors should not always assume that early treatment termination is a problem or sign that the client is at risk for relapse.

Relationship and Social Support Variables

Relationship and social support factors impact compliance. These include problems with family, friends, or other significant individuals. In addition, an unstable living situation or poverty can affect compliance.

Negative Social Supports

Negative social networks and relationships affect compliance behaviors. Clients who live or regularly socialize with others actively abusing alcohol or other drugs often feel pressure to use substances and are at high risk for poor compliance as well as relapse, particularly if they lack coping skills to deal with social pressures to use. A client who lacks family or other emotional supports for staying sober may have difficulty following through with treatment.

Family Problems

Negative family interactions can affect the client's motivation to change, to stay sober, and to attend treatment sessions or self-help groups. In some instances, family members object to, or directly sabotage, the client's participation in treatment. For example, during marital arguments, the wife of an alcoholic reminded him of his past transgressions while drinking, suggested he get drunk because she couldn't stand him sober, and verbally berated him to the point that he became angry and resentful. Unfortunately, his way of coping with these feelings was to pull back from his recovery plan and to isolate from people who supported his recovery. This, in turn, led to a relapse, as he had decreased his involvement in both counseling and self-help meetings. His decrease in compliance clearly resulted from angry feelings toward his wife that were precipitated by her negative attacks.

Unstable Living Situation/Poverty and Homelessness

Clients who lose stable living situations or are frequently forced to move from one environment to the next often are poorly compliant with treatment. Many homeless individuals, for example, have serious alcohol or other drug problems, mental illness, or both. Worrying about survival often takes precedence over treatment or attendance at self-help meetings for these clients.

Treatment and System Variables

Therapists and counselors often think that relationship factors are the main ones affecting a client's desire or ability to comply with professional treatment or self-help programs. Treatment system and caregiver factors such as the therapeutic alliance, attitudes, and abilities of counselors; access to treatment; and the type, expense, and duration of treatment also may impact compliance. Treatment programs and counselors or therapists can either enhance compliance or contribute to poor compliance in numerous ways.

Therapeutic Alliance

The therapeutic relationship, or working alliance, is crucial to working successfully with clients who have substance abuse disorders.[4] The client is likely to show displeasure in a problematic therapeutic alliance by missing sessions, by coming late or dropping out prematurely, or by failing to follow the agreed-on treatment plan. These problems are more likely to occur if the client believes that the counselor is authoritarian; perceives the counselor as not helpful; feels the counselor is neither empathetic nor optimistic about positive change; feels the counselor is judgmental, angry, disinterested, detached, or permissive; or feels the counselor is not an ally in the struggle to overcome alcohol or other drug problems and to achieve treatment goals.

On the other hand, counselors who are late for sessions or cancel appointments are likely to contribute to clients' dropping out of treatment early. A good working alliance allows the client to express thoughts, feelings, and struggles and makes the client feel understood, accepted, respected, and cared for, despite the problems that brought him or her to treatment in the first place. While at times clients may express thoughts or feelings about the counseling relationship to the counselor, more often they express themselves through their behaviors, such as missing counseling appointments, failing to complete therapeutic assignments, or dropping out of treatment prematurely.

Friendliness of Treatment Staff

Any member of a treatment program, from the counselor to the physician to the secretary, can have a negative impact on clients if he or she displays unhelpful, uncaring, or rude attitudes or behaviors. In our clinic satisfaction surveys, many clients report that the friendly and helpful attitude of various staff members was one of the most important factors in making them feel welcome. During a period in which we hired a temporary clinic secretary, several clients complained that they felt this secretary treated them rudely or indifferently. This example shows how any staff member, directly or indirectly, can affect how a client feels about coming to a clinic or treatment program. While some clients may verbalize their complaints to a counselor, most won't say anything directly. Negative feelings toward any staff member can influence a decision to miss sessions or stop treatment.

Demands on the Counselor

Budget cuts and increased demands on counselors can affect morale, motivation, and behavior toward clients. Counselors are not immune from anxiety and burnout associated with the changing environment in clinical care. Managed care, for example, has resulted in significant changes in length of treatment and reimbursement rates, which, in turn, impact the attitudes of counselors and clinic staff. Increased pressure to provide short-term, focused treatment makes it difficult to form long-term relationships with clients.

Competence of Staff

The training and competence of staff members of a treatment program can play a major role in a client's compliance with treatment. More experienced and knowledgeable counselors are often able to identify and resolve problems in the therapeutic relationship or with compliance early in the treatment process. They are also better at detecting other clients' problems such as psychiatric illness that impede recovery from a substance use disorder and that contribute to compliance problems. The client who perceives that the counselor is not competent in dealing with his or her problems may decide that treatment is not going to be effective and drop out.

Supervision of Staff

Inadequate supervision or monitoring of counseling staff can contribute to difficulties in client compliance. One of the roles of a supervisor is to help counselors address common problems encountered in clinical practice including impasses in the therapeutic relationship, negative feelings toward the client, and inappropriate behaviors or clinical interventions on the part of the counselor. Counselors with poor client compliance rates often blame "difficult" or "unmotivated" clients rather than look at how their own behaviors and attitudes might affect the client's use of treatment. For example, clients become very angry and upset when their counselor is late for sessions and makes them wait, especially if they are not informed as to the reason for the lateness. While clients usually understand that there are occasional emergencies or crises that require the counselor's immediate attention and will contribute to lateness, chronic patterns of lateness are distressing and less acceptable. Sometimes, clients complain to the counselor or clinic director. However, it isn't uncommon for the client whose counselor has difficulty keeping on schedule to simply lose interest in treatment, go elsewhere, or drop out without first trying to resolve the problem with the counselor. Supervision can address this and similar counselor problems so that the likelihood of negatively affecting a client is reduced.

Access to Treatment Evaluation

The ease or difficulty with which a client gains access to an initial evaluation or participation in a specific program impacts compliance. Usually, the longer a client has to wait for an evaluation after the initial phone contact, the greater the likelihood that he or she will miss this appointment and not enter treatment.[5]

Clients who initiate a telephone call requesting help and who then are transferred between several people before being given an appointment, or told that someone will call them back, may lose heart and change their minds about following through with the evaluation. Clients who complete a residential treatment program and then have to wait weeks or longer for follow-up counseling may lose interest and motivation in their aftercare plan.

Characteristics of Treatment Setting

The hours that a program operates, convenience of location, overall atmosphere, treatment philosophy, and actual services offered all can affect client compliance. Clients who work during the day need access to evening or weekend appointments. In some rural areas, treatment resources are limited and clients may have difficulty getting to sessions because of the distance they have to travel or because of transportation problems.

Type of Treatment Offered and Choices Available

Clients need to feel they have choices in the treatment services offered to them. For example, many clients complain about treatment programs that only offer group sessions. These clients feel cheated when they don't receive individual counseling. Many need individual sessions to self-disclose personal thoughts, feelings, and problems, which is a necessary process to facilitate change. If clients believe treatment isn't helping them, they're prone to dropping out. Clients sometimes express specific ideas on types of counseling. We have had clients, for example, who stated clearly during the initial session that they did not want counseling that was based on the Twelve Step model or that emphasized spirituality issues. On the other hand, we've had clients request counseling that focused on the Twelve Steps and a counselor in recovery from addiction. Counselors who are versatile and able to provide different types of interventions will be better equipped to adapt their treatment to the client.

Duration of Treatment Regimen

While short-term outpatient treatment has been shown to be effective with alcohol problems, to date there is no evidence that short-term treatment is effective with other types of drug abuse or dependency.[6] Studies sponsored by the National Institute on Drug Abuse indicate that these clients need at least three months of outpatient treatment before showing improvement.[7] As managed care organizations fund fewer admissions, less time in inpatient or residential treatment programs, and a limited number of outpatient sessions, counselors and clients alike express concern that shortened time in treatment leads to a number of problems that affect compliance. One client, for example, discharged from an inpatient rehabilitation program after only nine days stated: *Even before I went back to rehab I knew I needed more time than my insurance company would pay for. I was just beginning to feel better physically when I was discharged and admitted to an intensive outpatient program. I knew I needed the help, but my desire to use was so strong, I couldn't fight it off. Since I went back to the drugs, I didn't see any point in staying in treatment.*

Intensity of Treatment Program

Clients may become poorly compliant when they feel treatment is too intense or not intense enough to help them with their problems. Counseling professionals may recommend high levels of care such as residential, partial hospital, or intensive outpatient programs when, in reality, clients aren't interested in this intense level of treatment at the time of assessment. Despite this reluctance, the client may initially accept the recommendations of the counselor, then have inconsistent program attendance or drop out early. On the other hand, some programs may offer minimal treatment such as weekly or biweekly sessions when clients feel they need treatment several times per week or more. Some outpatient programs offer limited services due to lack of resources; as a result, clients do not receive the intensity of treatment they feel they need to recover.

Appropriateness of Treatment Recommendations

A client may be given several different recommendations only to have trouble complying because they are too overwhelming, complex, or difficult to follow. For example, Carl—a client with a mood disorder, a personality disorder characterized by aggressive and inappropriate outbursts, and alcoholism and marijuana abuse—was given a prescription for a mood stabilizer and an antidepressant. His counselor told him to attend group and individual therapy twice weekly, AA meetings at least three times per week, and a mental health support group for individuals with mood disorders. In addition, Carl was given multiple readings and journal assignments. While each treatment recommendation had a sound rationale from the point of view of the counselor, Carl felt that he had far too much to do and became demoralized because he couldn't keep up with all the demands placed on him. Since he couldn't comply with the numerous requests of his counselor, he felt guilty and blamed himself for not being motivated enough to recover. In addition to addressing his addiction and mental health problem, Carl had a family and a job. The excessive treatment and recovery demands clearly overwhelmed him.

Medication-Related Problems

A number of problems connected with taking medication for a substance abuse disorder, a psychiatric disorder, or both, can impact compliance. First, clients are sometimes reluctant to take medications because of the stigma associated with medications or the illness for which the medication is being used. Second, taking a medication for a psychiatric disorder is difficult for clients struggling to accept the reality of their illness. Third, clients who have unrealistic expectations of the role of medications may be disappointed if they don't receive immediate or significant benefits. Fourth, certain medications used for alcohol problems such as Antabuse cause an aversive reaction in the client who drinks alcohol while on this medication. Fifth, clients sometimes worry that they are not really "sober or clean" if they take certain types of medications, including some used to treat specific types of psychiatric symptoms. Sixth, psychiatric medications used to treat clients with dual disorders can have an adverse interaction with alcohol or illicit drugs used to get high. And, finally, side effects can be uncomfortable, intolerable, and not worth the effort for some clients. For example, side effects such as nausea, increased anxiety, or reduction of sexual libido have caused clients to stop taking their medications. In some instances, medications used to treat one disorder can trigger symptoms of another.

Expense of Treatment

Although many individuals will spend thousands of dollars or even much more on alcohol or other drugs, often they will not spend much of their own money on professional treatment. Clients who have to pay for part or all of the cost of treatment may stop going to sessions because they cannot afford the help or they simply don't want to spend their money on professional counseling or a treatment program.

Ineffective or Minimally Effective Treatment

If clients participate in treatment and follow the recommendations, yet show little or no improvement, they are at risk to reduce compliance or stop treatment completely. This is true with psychological or psychosocial treatments as well as with medications. If, for example, a cocaine addict participates in weekly outpatient therapy, but is unable to break the cycle of addiction and initiate a drugfree state, another treatment approach is clearly needed such as a more intensive outpatient program, a partial hospital program, or residential treatment. If dual-disordered clients agree to take medications to alleviate specific psychiatric symptoms, but experience little or no relief, they are likely to stop taking the medications. In some instances, when clients feel no improvement after a trial of medications, they stop participating in counseling as well.

Continuity of Care

When a client is discharged from a residential addiction treatment program or an inpatient dual disorders program, continuity of care is important to maintain gains and to address ongoing problems and treatment needs. When clients are placed on a waiting list for weeks or longer to enter the next phase of treatment, their desire for ongoing treatment may diminish.

Clients may fail to follow up with aftercare for a variety of reasons. We know of cases in which individuals have been given a limited supply of medications upon hospital discharge. If they canceled or missed their initial counseling appointment, then they would run out of medications, which contributed to a worsening or return of psychiatric symptoms. Loss of one's counselor and a shift to an unknown person can also disrupt continuity of care and reduce compliance.

Availability of Other Services

Clients with alcohol or other drug problems, as well as psychiatric disorders, also have practical or life problems to deal with. These problems will require help from other resources such as case managers, social service professionals, and vocational counselors. When other resources cannot be accessed and needs aren't met, the result can be partial or noncompliance with treatment.

Chart 4
Factors Affecting Compliance

Client Variables	*Illness- and Symptom-RelatedVariables*	*Relationship and Social Support Variables*	*Treatment and System Variables*
• Motivation • Beliefs • Stigma • Expectations • Satisfaction with Treatment • Personality • Other Addictions or Compulsions (gambling, smoking, etc.) • Other Life Events or Problems	• Symptoms of Addiction • Symptoms of Psychiatric Illness • Social Anxiety • Obsessions or Cravings to Use Substances • Previous History of Illness and Relapse • Failure to Catch Early Warning Signs of Relapse • Improvement in Symptoms or Problems	• Negative Social Supports • Family Problems • Unstable Living Situation/ Poverty and Homelessness	• Therapeutic Alliance • Friendliness of Treatment Staff • Demands on the Counselor • Competence of Staff • Supervision of Staff • Access to Treatment Evaluation • Characteristics of Treatment Setting • Type of Treatment Offered and Choices Available • Duration of Treatment Regimen • Intensity of Treatment Program • Appropriateness of Treatment Recommendations • Medication-Related Problems • Expense of Treatment • Ineffective or Minimally Effective Treatment • Continuity of Care • Availability of Other Services

Chapter 4

Effects of Compliance Problems

Introduction

Difficulty with compliance has an adverse impact on the client, family members, treatment professionals, and treatment systems. Other agencies or systems are affected as well. Poor compliance often leads to relapse, which, in turn, increases the risk of a variety of medical or psychosocial problems and the likelihood that other medical or social service systems will need to become involved with the client. Even payors (private as well as public sector) are affected as they ultimately fund services needed to address the problems that worsen or result from poor treatment compliance. With budgets shrinking and funds being scrutinized more closely by managed care organizations, poor treatment compliance has tremendous negative implications. In this chapter, we address common effects of compliance problems from the perspectives of the client, family, and caregiver systems.

Effects on the Client

The goals of substance abuse treatment are primarily to help clients initiate and maintain abstinence from alcohol or other drugs. In addition, treatment helps clients address problems contributing to or resulting from substance abuse or dependency and make specific personal or lifestyle changes. Treatment of dual disorders has similar aims with the additional goal of remission of, or significant improvement in, psychiatric symptoms. In cases involving chronic forms of psychiatric illness, treatment also aims to help the client learn to accept, live with, and manage persistent symptoms of illness that may wax and wane over time. Difficulty with compliance can interfere with any of these treatment goals. Thus, the client is less likely to receive the full benefits of treatment if he or she fails to attend sessions, take medication as prescribed, and complete agreed-on therapeutic assignments aimed at facilitating change.

A common outcome of poor treatment compliance is an increased likelihood of a lapse or relapse to alcohol or other drug use. The client who does not regularly attend treatment sessions and/or self-help programs and who lacks coping strategies is at greater risk to experience difficulty handling cravings to use. This client will also experience difficulty dealing with the external pressures (e.g., people, places, and things) and internal pressures (e.g., thoughts of using substances, negative thoughts about recovery, upsetting emotional states) that frequently contribute to resumption of substance use after a period of sobriety.

Symptoms of the dual-disordered client's psychiatric illness may worsen due to poor compliance with medications, therapy, or the treatment plan. For example, Lorraine, a sober drug addict whose recurrent major depression was in remission for over three years, stopped taking her antidepressants without first discussing this decision with her therapist or psychiatrist. As a result, Lorraine experienced a recurrent episode of major depression. It isn't unusual for some clients to show excellent compliance for a long time, only to make a poor decision during the maintenance phase of treatment.

Among substance-abusing clients with an additional psychiatric illness, poor compliance can also influence judgment and contribute to further clinical deterioration. For example, clients with bipolar illness, such as Bob, find that their judgment becomes impaired following exacerbation of manic symptoms, causing them to make foolish decisions and engage in harmful behaviors. Bob's poor compliance with lithium and subsequent erratic attendance at AA meetings led to family arguments and considerable distress. After ten years of remission from symptoms of bipolar illness and continuous sobriety from alcohol, Bob spent a large amount of the family's savings and decided to leave his wife of twenty-five years. Once he stopped complying with treatment and AA meetings, he went downhill rapidly.

Compliance problems leading to dropping out of treatment completely or leading to a return or worsening of symptoms increase the odds that the client will need a more expensive and higher level of care, such as inpatient hospitalization. The results of numerous research studies of clients who have alcohol or other drug problems show a powerful association between dropping out of treatment and a negative outcome.[1] For example, in a study we conducted on one of our inpatient units with dual diagnosis clients who had substance abuse or dependency and schizophrenia or a major mood disorder, over 60 percent of the clients identified poor compliance with abstinence and psychiatric medications as a major factor causing them to eventually return to the hospital.[2] These clients were able to see the effects of their poor compliance on psychiatric rehospitalization. In one of the studies we conducted in our outpatient clinic, we found that clients discharged from the hospital and referred to our outpatient program who failed to appear for their initial appointment were at considerable risk for rehospitalization.[3] In a related study of treatment participation during the first month of outpatient care following psychiatric hospitalization for dual diagnosis clients, we found that poorly compliant clients who failed to finish one month of outpatient treatment and dropped out of treatment early were six times more likely to be rehospitalized than those who were compliant and able to complete the first month of outpatient care.[4] Our research findings and clinical experience as well as numerous other studies clearly indicate that poor compliance raises the likelihood of clinical deterioration as well as the risk of rehospitalization for dual diagnosis clients.[5]

Medical problems often result from changes in clinical condition following poor treatment compliance. For example, the alcoholic with diabetes is less likely to comply with the plan to control this disease and more likely to experience medical complications as a result.

Substance abusers frequently report psychological problems such as lowered self-esteem and feelings of hopelessness following relapses or periods of poor compliance with their treatment plan. They feel guilty and shameful and often judge themselves harshly. Counselors sometimes convey negative expectations of clients. Some even feel incapable of making positive changes in their lives as a result of such expectations from self or counselors.

Family conflicts, lost relationships, and emotional turmoil may occur as a result of poor compliance with treatment. We frequently hear family members express anger, frustration, worry, fear, and confusion when their loved one relapses or is poorly compliant with treatment. Even in cases in which the client has not yet used alcohol or other drugs, or psychiatric symptoms have not recurred, family members intuitively know that poor compliance raises the odds of something negative happening, both with the client and the family.

Clients often report many other adverse effects of poor compliance with professional treatment or their personal recovery plan such as losing stability in a living situation, losing jobs, experiencing legal difficulties, getting incarcerated, feeling suicidal or acting on such feelings, acting out in violent ways in interpersonal relationships, falling into debt, and feeling spiritually bankrupt. While these are some of the most commonly reported negative effects of poor compliance, there are many others as well.

Poor compliance leading to resumption of substance use also raises the risk of the client's becoming involved in high-risk behaviors associated with HIV transmission or acquisition. Among IV drug users, behaviors such as sharing needles, cotton, or rinsing water are common. Sexual promiscuity and failure to practice safe sex are also common high-risk behaviors among clients with alcohol or other drug problems. While these behaviors sometimes continue despite the client's being sober, they are more common during periods of active substance use. For example, Wyatt, a gay man in recovery from addiction and multiple psychiatric disorders, became poorly compliant with outpatient treatment following a relapse to drug use. This, in turn, led to his visiting porno shops and engaging in unprotected, anonymous sex with other men, creating a risk of becoming HIV-positive or acquiring a sexually transmitted disease.

Although negative effects of poor compliance are common, in some instances clients report that problems associated with poor compliance may eventually have a positive impact on their motivation, commitment to treatment, or commitment to closely follow a personal plan for recovery. Following lapses or relapses, clients may reevaluate themselves and their approach to recovery, resulting in a renewed commitment to comply with their treatment plan. Of course, there is never any guarantee that a client who has relapsed to substance abuse or experienced a recurrence of psychiatric illness will benefit from this experience and change his or her compliance behaviors. There is always the risk that greater deterioration will occur. Nonetheless, for some clients, compliance and relapse problems do provide opportunities to learn from mistakes and rethink the approach taken in recovery.

Effects on the Family

Adverse effects of substance abuse and dual disorders on the family are well documented.[6] Poor compliance frequently causes concern among family members, particularly when the client relapses to substance abuse, has a recurrent episode of psychiatric illness, exhibits self-destructive or odd behaviors, or functions less effectively. Even if symptoms haven't yet returned, family members may worry about the possibility of relapse because they know what can happen when the client does not comply with treatment.

Family members often report feelings of anger, frustration, worry, and fear when a loved one is not compliant with the treatment plan. When the person with the problem refuses family efforts to help get him or her back on track and to comply with treatment, the family may feel incompetent or inadequate. Family members sometimes feel responsible when things go wrong, leading to self-blame. Situations in which poor compliance leads to a serious relapse may cause the family to feel hopeless or helpless. Family members may then give up on the client, especially in cases in which the family has previously experienced the relapses of a loved one.

Effects on Professional Caregiver or Treatment System

Professionals providing treatment experience feelings similar to the client's family: anger, worry, frustration, and hopelessness. They may also blame and judge the client and believe the client isn't capable of changing or benefiting from treatment. Some professionals even give up as they feel their efforts aren't worth it. Poor compliance among clients can even have an adverse impact on the morale of the caregivers who work hard at trying to help clients with substance use problems. The client may be terminated from treatment because of poor compliance. If the client later decides to return to treatment, the professional or agency may create barriers to block his or her return.

Poor compliance among clients may also have a detrimental effect on the treatment system as the clinic won't be reimbursed for clinical hours lost when clients fail to show for appointments. In the current age of managed care in which clinics or treatment programs are sometimes reimbursed only for actual direct service hours provided, revenue is lost. This, in turn, can jeopardize the agency because if sufficient revenues are not generated to cover costs, services may be discontinued. Or, agencies may be forced to lay off staff, which leads to the additional problem of the agency's having to "do more with less," creating another series of stressors on counselors and other caregivers.

Poorly compliant clients and/or their families frequently call professional caregivers during times of crisis asking for help. While the outcome may be favorable in terms of helping the client reenter treatment, the current crisis is usually complex and severe, and the time and energy expended by busy clinicians to help solve the problem can take a toll. For example, one counselor reported spending considerable time on the telephone talking to a poorly compliant client and her family. This client had stopped taking psychiatric medications, resumed alcohol use, and become suicidal. Her family was quite concerned, particularly since she refused to seek help for her relapse. The client reluctantly talked to the counselor who tried to persuade her to go to the psychiatric emergency room for an evaluation for possible inpatient admission. After several phone conversations with the client, the family, and the hospital, the counselor was finally able to make arrangements acceptable to the client. Again, while the clinical outcome was successful in helping a client in crisis reenter treatment, the time spent by the clinician was not reimbursed.

Poorly compliant clients are more likely to experience clinical as well as medical or psychosocial crises. Treatment systems are often faced with the challenge of locating suitable treatment or other resources needed to stabilize the current crisis. These clients are more likely than others to use more expensive services as well, such as emergency room evaluations, medical detoxification, or inpatient psychiatric treatment. As treatment monies are more closely monitored and controlled by managed care organizations, treatment systems that use a disproportionate amount of limited monies on higher levels of care will not be able to provide adequate services to other clients who need services.

PART two

Counseling and Systems Strategies to Improve Compliance

Chapter 5

Counseling Strategies to Improve Compliance

Introduction

A variety of counseling strategies have been shown to have a positive impact on client compliance.[1] These strategies relate to the following important areas:

- The *process of therapy* involves attending to the working alliance or therapeutic relationship, negotiating treatment goals, facilitating client participation in the treatment process, facilitating the client's discussion of concerns regarding the counselor or any aspect of treatment, and monitoring the client's compliance with medication in cases involving pharmacotherapy.
- The *content of therapy* involves monitoring substance abuse issues, monitoring psychiatric symptoms in cases of dual disorders, and providing education to clients and families.
- *Relationships with family members or significant others* involves eliciting the help of individuals who can support the client's interest in entering treatment and participating in an ongoing fashion.

This chapter discusses counseling strategies in detail to improve compliance. (See chart 5, page 83, for a comprehensive list of counseling strategies.) The counselor can also impact client compliance by facilitating the use of community programs that address specific problems or concerns of the client, such as the need for housing or vocational training. Chapter 6 will focus on ways in which the counselor can facilitate the use of other services on the client's behalf.

Express Empathy and Concern

Clients are more likely to develop a therapeutic alliance if they feel heard, understood, respected, and accepted by the counselor, regardless of the substance abuse history and related behaviors or attitudes. Clients who feel that they are working with the counselor as a team with the same goals, and who feel the counselor is optimistic about their ability to make changes, are likely to benefit from treatment and show better compliance with session attendance and completion of therapeutic assignments. The counselor can facilitate the alliance by changing any negative beliefs and attitudes toward the substance-abusing client and striving hard to understand what the client's life is actually like. If a client is late or misses sessions, or fails to carry out a therapeutic task, the counselor can examine these behaviors from the client's experience to determine reasons for the poor compliance. If a client is violent, indifferent to hurting others, or only mildly interested in changing his or her substance use, the counselor can view things from the client's perspective to gain an understanding of the reasons for these behaviors.

Convey Helpfulness in Attitudes and Behaviors

Conveying helpfulness involves adapting the counseling process to the problems and needs of the client rather than expecting the client to adapt to the treatment "program" or "approach." Being "client centered" means flexibility in developing and working toward treatment goals, determining the frequency and focus of counseling sessions, and determining involvement in other recovery activities such as self-help programs.

Accept and Appreciate Small Changes

The counselor also conveys helpfulness by not giving up on difficult clients and accepting small changes as a sign of progress. This is especially relevant for clients with a long history of severe dependency on alcohol or other drugs as well as those with severe psychiatric disorders. What seems like a small change for one client may be very significant for another. For example, a client who finally agrees to attend a few self-help meetings or talk with a physician regarding the use of medications is making a small but significant change.

Accept Ambivalence as Normal

Clients with an alcohol or other drug problem often initiate treatment as a result of external pressure from an employer, a family member, or the legal system. Thus, these clients are ambivalent about addressing their substance use problem and changing it, even in cases where the external pressures are great and the consequences of continued substance use can be severe such as loss of a job or significant relationship. Ambivalence shows in many ways; at times, clients will be very motivated and committed to the change process. During this time, compliance is usually better than during the times in which clients do not feel committed to changing. At other times, client ambivalence shows in erratic or poor compliance with sessions or not following the treatment plan. Their motivation may be low and they may not care much about the consequences of their behaviors. Their enthusiasm for treatment may wax and wane. One part of the client may want to continue treatment while another part may want to quit.

Ambivalence is especially common in the early stages of the change process and counselors should encourage clients to deal with their feelings. In an early recovery treatment group for new clients conducted in our clinic, the issue of mixed feelings (i.e., ambivalence) about coming for treatment sessions is commonly identified by the majority of clients, including those who initiated treatment on their own and not at the advice of someone else. While at times clients initiate a discussion on their ambivalence, the counselor facilitates such discussion by routinely introducing this topic in group discussions. As one client stated: *It was difficult to relate to a discussion on ways to change my lifestyle so I wouldn't continue using drugs when I wasn't even sure if I wanted to come back to this program for counseling. I had to convince myself I wanted to change first.*

Accept Varying Levels of Readiness to Change

The counselor needs to understand and accept that clients will be in various stages of readiness to change. For example, studies of problem drinkers show that many enter treatment because of psychosocial problems rather than a desire to quit drinking.[2] The lower the motivation and readiness to change, the less likely the client is to comply with a plan to change, particularly if the counselor tries hard to impose a change plan on the client. While clients may comply superficially, they are not likely to enjoy long-term benefits of treatment and change behaviors until they see the benefits of changing.

Anticipate Noncompliance at Various Stages of Treatment

The counselor can anticipate noncompliance at various stages of the change process, not only in the beginning stages. The client's motivation and ability to change are likely to vary over time. The motivation of clients with a well-established foundation of sobriety may change following a crisis or a period in which they feel increasingly bored or dissatisfied with their lives, despite being continuously sober. Clients with stable recovery who manifest problems in compliance with professional treatment or any aspect of their recovery plans are at risk for a relapse. It is easy for the client as well as the counselor to ignore potential warning signs based on the client's successful recovery. Yet many clients have relapsed because compliance-related indicators were ignored or shrugged off as being unimportant.

Discuss the Client's Prior History of Compliance

For clients who previously participated in professional treatment and recovery activities, reviewing the past history of compliance can help identify the various factors involved in poor compliance, early warning signs, and the impact of poor compliance on them and their families. A review of prior experiences allows the client to take a "failure" experience and make it a "learning" experience. This also helps the client identify aspects of treatment and recovery that were helpful. Some clients resist exploring past experiences and prefer focusing on the present. However, a review of past experiences can be instructive for the client. Sometimes needs have changed and the client may benefit from new and different recovery strategies.

Discuss Current Compliance Problems Immediately

The counselor can address compliance problems as soon as they arise in the treatment process. Late or missed sessions, partial or noncompliance with medications, poor self-help group attendance, or failure to complete recovery-oriented assignments should be discussed immediately to determine reasons for the client's behavior and to establish strategies to improve compliance or address ambivalence. Otherwise, the client may perceive that there is little or no accountability in treatment. Or, the client may perceive that the therapist isn't accountable either.

Provide Aftercare Compliance Counseling Prior to Discharge from Residential or Inpatient Care

Many clients who appear motivated to change as a result of participating in an intensive residential treatment program fail to follow through with aftercare treatment and subsequently relapse. Transitions from one level of care to another represent a major change for clients whether or not they recognize this. Clients who feel they've gained quite a bit from residential treatment may believe their problem is under control and not fully appreciate how difficult it can be in the real world to face the nuts-and-bolts demands of ongoing sobriety, such as dealing with cravings, desires, or social pressures to use substances; managing boredom, anger, depression, and other uncomfortable feelings; or dealing with conflictual relationships. Focusing on the differences between residential and community-based sobriety can provide the counselor an opportunity to increase clients' interest in aftercare. Chapter 9 provides a counseling model that we have found effective in improving compliance rates with the initial outpatient/aftercare appointment following hospital discharge.[3]

Help the Client Anticipate Roadblocks to Change

Roadblocks refer to barriers to the change process that make it difficult for the client to gain the maximum benefits from treatment or recovery. Roadblocks contribute to poor compliance and sabotage efforts to make positive changes. These fall into several categories:[4] attitudinal and motivational roadblocks (e.g., difficulty accepting problems, distrust of the counselor, low desire to change); personality roadblocks (e.g., impulsivity, stubbornness); interpersonal roadblocks (e.g., living with a partner who abuses drugs or alcohol); or lifestyle roadblocks (e.g., lack of structure in daily life or too much free time). Helping the client identify personal roadblocks or behaviors that sabotage recovery enables him or her to develop strategies to address these.

Encourage Discussions of the Counseling Process

Asking clients to discuss their thoughts or concerns about the counseling process or the counselor opens the door for early identification of problems that could contribute to poor compliance and early treatment dropout. This can be done periodically in counseling or whenever the counselor perceives a problem in his or her relationship with the client or with the counseling process. Giving permission for clients to specifically express doubts, concerns, or negative thoughts can be helpful. For example, clients may feel more comfortable sharing their thoughts or experiences if the counselor says something like this: *Frank, we've had the chance to meet three times to discuss ways to handle your cocaine problem. I'm interested in hearing what this has been like so far. Are we discussing issues and problems that are important to you? Do you feel your problems are listened to and that we are working together to find solutions? Even if you have criticisms of our work together, I'd like to know.* This gives the message that it is important to mutually review the counseling process and to address any problems immediately.

Encourage Discussions of the Client-Counselor Relationship

Although client-counselor relationship issues often get addressed when discussing how the counseling process is going, taking time to talk about the relationship with the client also opens the door to discussing important concerns and issues. *Carole, what do you think about how we are working together on your problems?* or *Carole, I'd like to give you the chance to talk about our counseling relationship. I'd like to know what you find helpful or if there's anything about our work together that you don't find helpful or would like to change.* Done in an open and nondefensive way, this conversation gives permission for the client to share thoughts, feelings, or concerns that may not otherwise be disclosed in the counseling process. Clients are likely to relate to the counselor in ways that are similar to how they relate to others. Interpersonal patterns or dynamics such as difficulty sharing feelings or a tendency to avoid conflicts may be addressed from this initial exploration.

Negotiate Rather Than Dictate Change Plans

In substance abuse treatment, clients are often told what to do in terms of attending self-help meetings, group counseling sessions, or other activities perceived to be in their best interest. While at times this directive stance may be helpful, in general, plans and methods to achieve change should be discussed and negotiated, even if the therapist disagrees with the client.

Ray, a client who was not interested in following his previous counselor's recommendation to attend AA meetings for a variety of reasons, had this to say about the negotiated change plan with a new counselor: *I've been in treatment and recovery a couple of times and I feel I really gave AA a chance. But it just didn't work for me, and I feel my reasons are legitimate. In the past, I've been told I wasn't motivated, or hadn't surrendered yet, and this was why I didn't accept AA. My new counselor surprised me by listening to my concerns about AA and accepting the fact that I just didn't feel AA was for me. We discussed all the pros and cons of AA and other self-help groups so I was well aware that there weren't a lot of alternatives. But we came up with an agreement that I would try Rational Recovery. I found this program to be helpful and attended regularly. It's like AA in that it isn't for everyone but having a choice on which self-help program to attend was very important to me.*

Ray is not unique in his need for a self-help program other than AA. While evidence is abundant that AA and other Twelve Step programs benefit many people with alcohol or other drug problems, alternatives are clearly needed for those who desire a different option for their recovery. Negotiating rather than dictating is likely to nurture the therapeutic alliance and promote compliance.

Emphasize the Client's Responsibility to Participate in Treatment

Ultimately, clients must take responsibility for the degree to which they participate in the treatment process. The counselor can offer the best treatment available, but it is up to the client to choose whether to participate, both in terms of complying with the actual sessions and actively applying what is learned in treatment to change their lives. If the counselor determines that the client is getting little or no benefit, a discussion can focus on the possible reasons for this as well as how the counselor and client can change their strategies in an attempt to increase treatment participation. Or, they mutually may decide to terminate treatment or explore other treatment options.

Emphasize the Client's Responsibility to Change

Although the counselor can facilitate change in the client by developing a positive working alliance and using a variety of clinical strategies, the client must accept responsibility to actually make specific personal or lifestyle changes. For example, a client can fully accept and understand that his recovery will be less volatile if he avoids certain people, places, or things associated with prior alcohol or drug use. Yet this client can fail to change his behaviors, continue to pursue high-risk people or places, and thereby put himself at risk for relapse. Ultimately, it is up to clients to take responsibility to translate change strategies into their daily lives.

Provide Education to the Client and Family

Education can help clients and families gain an understanding of substance abuse or dual disorders (symptoms, causes, effects), professional treatments available (psychosocial, medical, pharmacotherapeutic), the recovery process, stages of change, self-help programs, causes of relapse, and relapse prevention strategies. In addition, each client or family may have specific questions or concerns for which they need information. Educational interventions are nonthreatening and often pave the way for self-evaluation and self-awareness, which, in turn, facilitate actual change in the client. Education can easily be integrated into the treatment process. Many excellent educational materials (books, workbooks, videotapes, audiotapes) are available for counselors to use in providing education to clients and families.

Knowledge empowers and helps the client have a greater repertoire from which to choose in making decisions. For example, the client who has struggled with persistent and strong alcohol cravings may benefit from learning about medications such as ReVia or Antabuse, which can reduce cravings or increase confidence in the ability to abstain. Education also helps dispel myths about medications and negative perceptions that have resulted from these (e.g., "You shouldn't need to use a crutch in staying sober"). Education on motivational roadblocks or relapse warning signs can help clients become aware of common problems in recovery, thus giving them an opportunity to develop strategies to address these and not drop out of treatment during periods of low motivation or when struggling with a problem.

Provide Interventions Based on Empirical Support

There are several effective treatments for substance use and dual disorders. Many of these are described in clinical manuals that provide a theoretical framework as well as specific clinical strategies associated with the particular model of treatment.[5] By becoming familiar with the latest and most effective treatments, the counselor is better able to help clients. Less effective interventions can be changed as the counselor's knowledge and skill increase. For example, if research indicates that harsh confrontation is effective only with a small percentage of substance-abusing clients, and client-centered motivational interventions are effective with a large percentage of clients, it makes sense for counselors to learn about motivational strategies and to use these in counseling sessions. As more knowledge becomes available from empirical studies, the counselor can become better equipped to provide effective treatment. This implies an openness and willingness to consider new ideas and approaches to treatment. As managed care organizations play a more active role in authorizing and paying for treatment services, the need for empirically based interventions and outcome data on clinical work is more important than ever.

Elicit Family Support and Involvement

Many experts have written about the importance of family or significant-other involvement in assessment and treatment. Such involvement has been shown to improve rates of treatment entry and retention in the treatment of substance dependence.[6] Family members can provide important information that influences the treatment plan. They know the client well and can add additional history to that provided by the client. The client's family should be involved as soon as possible, ideally during the assessment process or the early phase of recovery. As part of the assessment process, the counselor can evaluate the effects of the client's substance use or dual disorders on the family, family reactions, the relationship between the client and family members, the degree of support the family can provide the client, and the client's perception of the concerns, worries, or questions of the family. During individual family sessions, the counselor can address the specific questions or concerns of family members. During multiple-family group sessions, the counselor can provide information to the family and elicit mutual support among different families experiencing similar problems. Involving the family members can also help them solve problems specific to their relationship with the substance abuser, learn behaviors to avoid (e.g., enabling, shielding the member from negative consequences of substance use, overfunctioning) and behaviors that are helpful (e.g., setting limits, taking care of their own needs, attending support groups with other families). In some instances, the counselor will need to refer family members for help with personal problems such as a mental health disorder, a substance use disorder, or another serious difficulty that requires professional assistance.

Explore the Client's Expectations, Hopes, and Goals for Treatment

Part of the counseling process involves discussing what the client hopes to gain from treatment, including specific goals and ways to meet these goals. It isn't unusual for the client to have expectations or goals for treatment that differ from those of the counselor. Expectations can be too high, too low, or unrealistic. If expectations are too high, the client may become disappointed when they are not met. If expectations are too low, the client may not engage as seriously and work as hard as is needed to make changes in substance use patterns. If expectations are too unrealistic, the counselor can be put in a position to fail. The client's goals may be different from what the counselor believes to be appropriate. At times, the client may be open to persuasion and change his or her goals. Other times, change is less likely. Major differences between the counselor and client related to expectations or goals can lead to compliance problems.

Regularly Review Treatment Goals and Progress

Regular review of treatment goals and progress toward those goals is essential. This process helps clients identify problems or issues they need to continue working on as recovery progresses. Reviewing progress also may encourage clients as they see the results of their efforts. For example, if clients feel frustrated with how things are going in their lives, yet see that they've been able to maintain abstinence despite their frustration, they may be less likely to give up on their recovery. They are then more likely to comply with treatment and their recovery plan during difficult periods.

Discuss the Pros and Cons of Treatment and Self-Help Programs

Professional treatment and participation in self-help programs take time, energy, and commitment on the part of the client. A cost-benefit analysis can help the client identify the pros and cons of involvement in recovery. If the advantages clearly outweigh the perceived disadvantages from the client's point of view, he or she is likely to show better compliance with treatment or participation in self-help programs.

The counselor cannot assume that each client enters treatment or self-help programs with an optimistic attitude or positive regard. We have found in our clinical practice that clients are more likely to comply with self-help programs if they choose to attend and if they have the opportunity to discuss any negative perceptions, reactions, or experiences resulting from past participation in such programs. If a client presents a strong negative experience or belief about AA or NA, yet is instructed to attend ninety meetings in ninety days, compliance is likely to be poor. One of the counselor's most difficult tasks is helping clients make their own decisions regarding ongoing recovery, especially when they are at odds with the counselor's beliefs about recovery or involvement in a self-help program.

Discuss the Pros and Cons of Abstinence

Clients with substance use disorders often do not see the need for total abstinence from all substances. Clients with cocaine dependency who occasionally smoke marijuana or drink alcohol in moderation may not see anything wrong with using these substances from time to time, especially if prior use has not caused problems. They may not worry that marijuana or alcohol use can increase their risk for cocaine relapse or lead to a dependency on these substances. Clients who are not dependent on alcohol or other drugs, but have some problem with their substance use, often see less of a need for total abstinence than those who are dependent. However, even clients diagnosed with an alcohol or other drug dependency problem may resist abstinence as their initial goal. This presents a challenge to the counselor who believes abstinence is a prerequisite for treatment. The counselor may push the client to accept abstinence before he or she is ready. Discussing the pros and cons of abstinence and continued substance use can help the client make the most informed decision regarding what needs to change and how to go about changing. While we don't promote substance use among those with dependency problems, we recognize that many clients will not initially accept our recommendation for total abstinence. Interestingly, clients who resist abstinence early in treatment often learn through experience that they cannot safely or consistently limit their substance intake over an extended period. Thus, they learn that "their way" does not work and that they need to change their beliefs about substance use, their treatment goals, and their recovery plan.

Provide Options Regarding Treatment

Following an initial assessment, the client can be given a menu of options regarding treatments that are available to address his or her substance use disorder. Treatment needs can be assessed using the levels-of-care criteria of the American Society of Addiction Medicine (ASAM).[7] ASAM delineates several levels of care from the least restrictive (e.g., outpatient) to the most restrictive (e.g., medically managed detoxification or rehabilitation) across six domains of functioning: intoxication and withdrawal potential; biomedical conditions and complications; psychological or emotional conditions and complications; treatment readiness; relapse potential; and recovery environment. ASAM criteria help to "match" the client to the most appropriate level of care based on a thorough assessment and to make recommendations unique to the clinical presentation of the client. While specific recommendations can and should be based on the counselor's evaluation, the client has the final say regarding the treatment option to pursue (unless there are external constraints, such as the client's having been mandated to attend treatment by an employer or legal system). In addition to providing the client with options regarding the level of care, length of the initial treatment contract, and frequency of treatment sessions, the counselor can also provide options regarding self-help programs that address substance use or dual disorders. Options provided will vary from one geographic area to the next, depending on availability. In rural areas and small towns, for example, self-help groups such as Women for Sobriety, Rational Recovery, Smart Recovery, or Dual Recovery Anonymous may not be available.

Change Treatment Frequency and Intensity

Treatment level intensity or frequency of sessions can be increased or decreased as the client's clinical condition or motivation improves or deteriorates. Regular review of the client's progress in treatment allows the counselor to arrange for a different level of care or change session frequency.

Clients often use fewer residential treatment days, partial hospital days, intensive outpatient days, or outpatient treatment sessions than are offered. When a client's situation changes and there is serious concern about the possibility of a relapse, or if the client does not seem to be benefiting from the current level of treatment, a higher level of care can be recommended. Oftentimes clients participate in a level of care that the counselor believes is not adequate to address the substance use disorder. In such cases, the counselor can negotiate for a higher level of care if certain benchmarks are not met (e.g., the client is unable to initiate abstinence within a certain period) or if certain behaviors occur (e.g., a relapse of moderate severity or greater following a period of abstinence). For example, Patrick, a client with heroin dependence and alcohol abuse, initially refused the counselor's recommendation for an intensive outpatient program following completion of a brief inpatient detoxification and stabilization program. It soon became clear that Patrick's program of weekly outpatient counseling was insufficient to address the serious nature of the addiction. Therefore, a higher level of care was strongly recommended to help him reestablish abstinence and begin dealing with the lifestyle problems caused by his drug dependence.

Provide Direct Feedback to the Client

Providing feedback to a client—telling the client how he or she is doing—is an important and potentially powerful clinical intervention. Feedback can relate to progress, compliance, or the counselor's observations of the client (i.e., the client's attitudes or behaviors in treatment sessions or between sessions). Feedback can be given when reviewing the treatment plan or provided spontaneously as part of the treatment process. For example, Mike, recovering from recurrent major depression and alcohol dependence, has been hospitalized several times for stabilization of severe mood symptoms and detoxification from alcohol. After Mike made a casual comment, indicating he was not very committed to aftercare treatment, his counselor gave him this feedback regarding his use of inpatient services: *In reviewing your drinking, depression, and past experiences in the hospital, Mike, I can see that you usually do pretty well for up to a couple of months after you are discharged. During this time, you follow your plan and attend outpatient counseling, take your medications as prescribed, and go to AA meetings regularly. Once you stop your medications, however, you usually hit the bottle again, and you quit going to meetings and counseling. Your depression gets worse and then your drinking gets out of hand. You become suicidal and end up back in the hospital. When you stick to your plan, even when things aren't going your way, you do much better. You're able to stay sober and deal with your depression. On the other hand, when you stop your plan you head downhill. Based on what you told me, I'm concerned that you won't follow through with treatment when you leave the hospital.*

Feedback needs to be direct, specific, objective, and nonjudgmental, and presented to the client in a timely manner. If clients are consistently late for treatment sessions and don't receive feedback on this behavior until after an actual relapse occurs, the counselor missed an opportunity to help these individuals to evaluate themselves and decide if they need to make a change.

Discuss the Client's Reactions to Feedback

It makes good clinical sense to ask clients for their thoughts and feelings about the feedback. Eliciting the client's reactions provides him or her with an opportunity to agree or disagree with the counselor's conclusions. In many instances, the client will agree and may find the feedback to be useful, even if initially hard to take.

Provide Reinforcement for Treatment Compliance

Reinforcement or rewards can be effective in motivating the client to continue with the treatment plan, particularly in relation to the goal of abstinence from substances. One type of reinforcement is to award clients with vouchers that can be exchanged for products or services. A number of recent studies have shown that clients with cocaine dependency who receive vouchers for producing negative urinalysis tests comply much better with the goal of abstinence than clients who do not receive such financial reinforcement.[8] While some counselors object to this strategy and view it as manipulation or "paying for sobriety," the argument can be made that any clinical intervention that helps clients initiate or maintain abstinence during the critical early months of treatment is worthwhile. Most community-based alcohol and drug abuse treatment clinics do not have the resources to provide elaborate reinforcements for compliance. However, small reinforcers such as free recovery literature, bus tickets, certificates for free lunch, or certificates for small items at a local discount store could be used to improve compliance with treatment session attendance, self-help meeting attendance, medication, or abstinence from alcohol or other drugs.

Address Anxiety about Treatment or Self-Help Group Attendance

Group therapy and self-help programs are commonly used to address substance use disorders. In one of our quality assurance/quality improvement studies of social anxiety and related avoidant behavior, significant numbers of our outpatients reported high levels of social anxiety regarding participating in groups or self-help meetings.[9] In addition, many also reported avoiding these and other social situations in which they felt a high degree of social anxiety. Even situations such as introducing oneself and talking before, during, or after an AA or NA meeting or reading the Twelve Steps or Twelve Traditions aloud to the AA or NA group can cause considerable anxiety and make some clients feel overwhelmed.

Despite the commonness of social anxiety and avoidant behaviors, some treatment programs rely heavily on groups and provide limited or no individual counseling. We have talked with more than one thousand clients over a period of several years as part of a regular review of our inpatient, partial hospital, and outpatient treatment programs and in reviewing other treatment programs in the United States and Europe. Clients have consistently told us that they strongly believe individual counseling is important to their recovery. While many of these clients feel group treatment is helpful, they believe that individual sessions are essential for discussing problems and concerns difficult to disclose in groups. Socially anxious clients are also more likely to miss group sessions than individual counseling sessions.

The counselor can assess each client to determine if social anxiety and avoidant behavior are problems that could affect group treatment or self-help program attendance. In cases in which anxiety is likely to reduce client participation, the counselor can provide education and counseling on strategies to reduce social anxiety and to work through feelings. Behavioral rehearsals or role-plays are excellent counseling techniques for helping the client become aware of thoughts and feelings associated with various social situations and in getting the client to practice dealing with social situations prior to experiencing them. Clients with more severe levels of social anxiety who do not respond to these or other counseling strategies are likely to have an anxiety disorder that may require specialized treatment. Many excellent treatments specifically designed for anxiety disorders are available.[10]

Monitor Substance-Abuse Recovery Issues

Monitoring the common issues faced by the client in recovery (e.g., cravings; desire to use; close calls; high-risk people, places, or events; motivation changes; boredom) is a way of identifying problems early and adjusting the change plan to address these problems.[11] Since clients in recovery are sometimes hesitant to self-disclose serious problems, upsetting thoughts or feelings, or other problems before a therapeutic alliance has formed, exploring these common issues in sessions helps the counselor determine how the client is doing and whether or not any change in the plan is needed. There is often a relationship between a client's struggling with a common recovery issue or task and noncompliance with the recovery plan.

Discuss Cravings and Thoughts of Using Substances

Cravings or thoughts about using alcohol or other drugs are common, especially during the early weeks and months of abstinence. Many internal and external factors trigger cravings and increase positive thoughts regarding substance use. Routinely discussing cravings, their intensity and frequency, potential triggers, the context in which they occur, and how they affect thinking aids the client in several ways. The client learns that cravings and thoughts of engaging in substance use are common in recovery. The client also learns to be aware when he or she is experiencing cravings. Monitoring cravings and thoughts of using on a regular basis helps the client see their connection to internal events, such as upsetting feelings or distorted thinking, and to external events, such as social pressures to drink or use drugs. In addition to regular discussions during counseling sessions, the counselor can have the client keep a daily log of cravings and thoughts of wanting to use substances. Keeping vigilant can enable the client to avert a relapse and potential reduction of compliance with the treatment program.

Identify People, Places, Events, and Close Calls

External events, situations, or relationships also impact the recovery process and, consequently, compliance. Involvement with high-risk events where substances are readily available or there is pressure to engage in substance use; or involvement with high-risk people such as drug dealers or active drug abusers raises the risk of relapse. Such involvement can have a negative impact on compliance before the client actually relapses or after substances are used again. In examining the relapse process of hundreds of clients, we found a similar pattern: they are faced with one or more high-risk events, situations, or interpersonal encounters, experience an increase in cravings or thoughts of using substances, reduce or stop involvement in professional treatment, or reduce or stop self-help program attendance. Often, though not always, clients quit complying with the goal of abstinence following a lapse or relapse. They think, "Why even bother since I relapsed," or "I'd like to fit in, and having a few (drinks, snorts, tokes) can't hurt me that much." The counselor can help the client identify high-risk people, places, and events by routinely inquiring about actual or potential "close calls." The client has the opportunity to discuss the actual impact of such situations on recovery and to acknowledge desires to use substances, fit in with other users, or enjoy activities or events associated with substance use.

Assess Motivation to Change

Motivation to change is a significant factor in complying with treatment sessions and the individualized recovery plan.

Clients who are motivated to change and work a specific recovery plan often do much better than those with low motivation. Motivated clients are likely to comply with scheduled counseling sessions or self-help group attendance. However, motivation to change often wavers, especially in the early weeks or months of recovery. A client can feel highly motivated to change one day, then poorly motivated the next. Even clients who have done well for a substantial period of time can experience changes in their level of motivation.

In general, clients don't spontaneously report significant changes in their motivation, so the counselor should periodically assess this. The counselor can initiate discussions to help determine internal or external factors that may be affecting the client's motivation. Reduced motivation may show in many ways, some obvious, others more subtle. These include, but are not limited to, the client's

- feeling bored with treatment
- feeling critical of the counselor or treatment program
- being late for sessions
- not completing therapeutic assignments
- feeling that there are no problems to work through
- worrying that he or she could go back to "old" behaviors (substance abuse and related behaviors)

Monitor Substance-Use Relapse Warning Signs

Warning signs often precede relapse to substance use following a period of sobriety.[12] Warning signs may be obvious (e.g., abruptly stopping attendance at self-help meetings), subtle (e.g., becoming critical of self-help programs, counselors, or recovery activities), or peculiar to a particular individual (e.g., significant increase in mental health symptoms such as depression or anxiety). Monitoring the client's relapse warning signs is another way of helping him or her remain vigilant about recovery. The client can take action to manage the warning signs before a substance-use relapse occurs. In examining the relapse process of many clients, we found that the appearance of relapse warning signs often coincides with changes in the client's ability to comply with treatment sessions and follow the change plan.

Monitor Psychiatric Symptoms

A helpful intervention for clients who have a psychiatric disorder in addition to a drug or alcohol problem is monitoring their major psychiatric symptoms, particularly in the early phases of recovery.[13] Symptoms of psychiatric illness such as poor judgment, hallucinations, low energy, or depressed mood can adversely influence motivation, decision making, and compliance with treatment. Psychiatric symptoms can also affect the client's compliance with abstinence from using alcohol or other drugs. Monitoring psychiatric symptoms is particularly helpful for clients with severe and persistent forms of psychiatric illness who have trouble self-disclosing their symptoms. These clients often need prompting by the counselor to report specific symptoms of their illness.

Address Persistent or Residual Psychiatric Symptoms

While some clients function relatively well between episodes of psychiatric illness, others never achieve full remission and experience persistent or residual symptoms. This is true whether or not the client is active in therapy or other forms of psychosocial treatment and takes medications for the psychiatric illness. For example, clients with schizophrenia, bipolar disorder, borderline and other personality disorders, chronic depression, or chronic anxiety often experience symptoms of their illness even during the course of active treatment. The counselor can help these clients by encouraging acceptance of the chronicity or persistence of the disorder and acceptance of the reality that some symptoms may always be present and by teaching clients to regularly monitor persistent symptoms in order to know when significant changes require professional consultation or a modification in the change plan.[14]

Monitor Psychiatric Relapse Warning Signs

Teaching dual diagnosis clients to monitor signs of relapse or recurrence of psychiatric illness can prepare them to take early action should symptoms worsen during treatment or return following a period of remission.[15] Many clients report that they failed to take action when psychiatric symptoms initially returned or worsened only to eventually experience a full-blown recurrence of their illness. As their symptoms worsened, judgment and motivation were adversely affected, leading to stopping or cutting down on therapy sessions or partial hospital program attendance, medications used to treat the psychiatric illness, or self-help program attendance, or not working their individualized recovery program. Often, reduced compliance led to further worsening of symptoms and the subsequent need for a higher level of care, especially when nothing was done about the change in compliance.

The counselor can teach the client general signs of recurrence. For example, changes in attitudes regarding members of the treatment team, the treatment program, a sponsor, or self-help programs; changes in attendance at self-help or treatment sessions; changes in daily habits; and changes in mood often precede relapse regardless of the specific psychiatric disorder. These behaviors may be quite obvious to the client or to significant others, or these changes may be subtle. In addition to general relapse warning signs, the therapist can teach the client illness-specific signs of relapse.[16]

While the process of relapse is similar across different disorders, indicators vary according to the particular psychiatric illness.

Consider the Use of Medications

Medications can help clients with alcohol or other drug problems, psychiatric illness, or both. A considerable amount of research indicates that medications can enhance the effectiveness of psychosocial treatments and that psychosocial treatments such as behavioral therapies alone are sometimes not sufficient in treating drug abuse or dependency.[17] Counselors can help clients to consider potential positive effects of medications to treat certain cases of alcohol or other drug dependency or psychiatric disorders among clients with dual disorders.

Following are some indications when medications can help the client in recovery from an alcohol or other drug dependency disorder as well as the client with an additional psychiatric illness.[18] The client

- has been unable to stay off of alcohol, tobacco, or other drugs for longer than a few months at a time;
- has tried other forms of treatment and still gone back to using alcohol, tobacco, or other drugs;
- feels it is very difficult to abstain from alcohol, tobacco, or other drugs despite knowing he or she should quit and wanting to quit;
- often feels overwhelmed by cravings and strong desires to use alcohol, tobacco, or other drugs;
- has a lot to lose if he or she relapses, such as an important relationship, job, or professional status or license;
- finds his or her physical health or mental stability increasingly affected the longer the substance use continues;

- believes his or her life would be better if he or she stayed sober from alcohol, tobacco, or other drugs; or
- believes medications will help him or her benefit more from other forms of treatment such as professional therapy or self-help groups.

Prepare the Client for Taking Medications

While professionals can easily identify many potential benefits to taking medications for a substance use disorder, psychiatric disorder, or both, clients often do not want to take medications for a variety of reasons. Intolerable side effects, lack of knowledge of the goals of taking medications, unrealistic expectations of what medication can and cannot do for the client, stigma associated with having to take medications, failure to accept diagnosis, disapproval from families or significant others, and distrust of the physician are common reasons for noncompliance or poor compliance with taking medications. In these instances, counselors can help clients by preparing them to take medications.

Preparing clients involves educating them on what medication they are taking, why they are taking it, how and when specific dosages are taken, implications of missed dosages, implications for mixing the medication with alcohol or other drugs, common or possible side effects, immediate and long-term beneficial consequences, how to know if the medication is effective, and when to call the counselor or physician with questions or concerns about the medication. Providing written instructions or educational booklets on specific medications is another excellent way to educate the client and family. The clinician and treatment team should be respectful of the client reluctant to take medication and be willing to work with him or her on the benefits of medications. For example, Marge, a nurse with major depression and alcohol dependence, stated that she did not want to take antidepressants and preferred a trial of outpatient therapy. Despite being continuously sober, her depressive symptoms improved only slightly and continued to cause personal suffering and difficulty functioning at work and home. She finally agreed to take medication for her depressive disorders, but only after she felt she had first given outpatient therapy a chance.

Monitor Medication Compliance

The counselor usually has more frequent contact with the client than the psychiatrist prescribing medications for a psychiatric disorder and is more likely to identify problems with medications that have serious potential consequences. Medication compliance can be monitored by regularly asking the client specific questions about whether or not all medication doses have been taken and ascertaining the reasons for missed doses. All sorts of unexpected events occur that can affect a client's decision to alter compliance with medications. For example, Jean, a woman with chronic depression, anxiety, and alcoholism and cocaine dependence, had been taking an antidepressant for several years. When she developed a specific medical condition, her primary care physician prescribed a medication to treat the condition. Because she feared the interaction of this medication with her psychiatric medication, Jean stopped taking her antidepressant for several weeks. The failure to discuss her concerns about medication interactions led to noncompliance, which, in turn, contributed to a return of her depressive symptoms.

Early in treatment the client should agree to call the counselor or psychiatrist before making a unilateral decision to stop taking medicine. Although the ideal situation is for the client to keep all scheduled appointments with the psychiatrist managing the medications, this doesn't always occur in clinics, which causes some clients to neglect refilling their prescriptions. The counselor can also ask the client to agree to call the clinic before prescriptions run out as it may take several days or longer to get the client an appointment with a physician who can write a renewal prescription. These types of agreements make it more difficult for the client to stop taking medications, while conveying a sense of client responsibility to consult with the treatment team before deciding to stop medications or let prescriptions run out.

Compliance with some psychiatric medications can also be monitored through laboratory tests that measure the level of a particular medication in the bloodstream. If a medication is below the range of therapeutic effectiveness, then either the dosage is too low or the client is not taking the medication as prescribed. The client may also be using substances that interact with the medication (e.g., alcohol can lower levels of antidepressants). If the medication level is too high, the client may be taking more than prescribed or a higher dosage than can be tolerated or using substances that increase the level of medication in the bloodstream.

Address Adverse Side Effects or Lack of Efficacy

Clients who are prescribed medications for psychiatric disorders should be provided education on potential side effects, efficacy, or effectiveness of these medicines, and length of time needed to affect symptoms. While some medication side effects are minor and remit over time, other side effects are more bothersome. Also, there is no guarantee that a specific medication will be effective with a specific client even if it has a high overall rate of effectiveness.

Clients can be instructed to talk with the counselor or treating psychiatrist should serious side effects occur or if little improvement is made after a sufficient period of time taking the medication. Unfortunately, some clients want immediate relief and stop medications if they don't experience quick results, even with medications such as antidepressants that often require two weeks or longer to show positive effects on symptoms.

Medication efficacy is an interesting issue. For one thing, medications that are generally effective won't necessarily work well for every client. Also, medications won't always be 100 percent effective since some clients will experience residual or persistent psychiatric symptoms even if they take adequate dosages. Clients with chronic and persistent forms of mental illness therefore need to be educated on how to gauge the success of a medicine. For example, Scott is a young man with chronic mental illness and addiction who experiences severe hallucinations, paranoia, and depression. He was prescribed antipsychotic and antidepressant medications. While the antipsychotic medications led to a significant improvement in psychotic symptoms, Scott continued to experience hallucinations, although they were less frequent, intense, and bothersome and interfered considerably less with his daily functioning. These medications were effective in that there was about a 70 percent symptomatic improvement in this client. The reality is that some clients will experience persistent symptoms regardless of whether or not they take adequate dosages of psychiatric medications.

Facilitate Medication Changes for Ineffective Medicines

Every client will not respond to medications in a similar fashion. There will be cases in which a particular medication shows little or no effect on the client's symptoms after an adequate trial. If a medication fails to have a positive impact on reducing psychiatric symptoms, another type of medication may be needed.

The counselor can facilitate a reevaluation of the medication regime in cases where medications are not effective. However, there are two issues for the counselor to consider. First, if the client continues to abuse alcohol or other drugs, then obtaining an accurate picture of efficacy of medications is very difficult since substances can adversely impact psychiatric medications. In such cases, the counselor should work with the client on sobriety issues so that he or she can gain maximum benefit from medications. Second, some clients with more chronic and persistent forms of mental illness will always experience some psychiatric symptoms and residual disability regardless of which medications they take. Sometimes these clients request a medication change any time their symptoms increase. While the counselor and psychiatrist want to be sensitive to the suffering of the client, they do not want to fall into the trap of making constant medication changes as this often does not lead to clinical improvement. In fact, too many medication changes can give the client the message that symptom changes are only dealt with through pharmacotherapy. As a result, the client may devalue therapy or other psychological or social interventions that are important to the overall recovery effort.

Facilitate Augmentation Therapy

While many clients benefit from a single medication to treat symptoms of a psychiatric disorder, others require augmenting the medication regime with an additional medication. Augmentation therapy is usually recommended if the client realizes some benefits from the medication but still experiences symptoms that are distressing or interfere with functioning. For example, Paul, a client with recurrent major depression and alcoholism, had tried several different antidepressants over the course of several years. Even the most effective antidepressant had only a modest impact on his depressive symptoms despite his continued abstinence from alcohol. His medication regime was augmented with lithium, which led to a marked improvement in his depressive symptoms and a significant reduction of recurrences of depression.

Prepare for Negative Reactions from Self-Help Group Members to Medications

Although considerable changes have occurred in the attitudes of self-help groups such as Alcoholics Anonymous, Narcotics Anonymous, and Cocaine Anonymous, some members of these programs continue to hold rigid beliefs regarding the use of medications for psychiatric disorders. They may believe a member is not really sober or clean if taking a medication. Or, they may believe that taking medications such as Antabuse, ReVia, or Trexan to help with sobriety are merely "crutches." In some instances, a member of a self-help group may aggressively try to persuade another member that the medications are not needed—that this member needs to "white-knuckle it," learn new coping strategies, and stop relying on "crutches" to aid recovery. Although Twelve Step fellowships do not advocate that members play the role of doctor and advise others on medications, in reality this sometimes occurs. The counselor can prepare clients to handle this issue should it arise. The client who reports anxiety regarding how to respond to pressures to stop taking medications can be taught, through role-plays, different ways of responding to such pressures. We have also found it helpful to provide written educational materials such as the booklet published by Alcoholics Anonymous World Services, Inc., entitled *The AA Member and Medications*.[19]

Chart 5
Counseling Strategies to Improve Compliance

- Express Empathy and Concern
- Convey Helpfulness in Attitudes and Behaviors
- Accept and Appreciate Small Changes
- Accept Ambivalence as Normal
- Accept Varying Levels of Readiness to Change
- Anticipate Noncompliance at Various Stages of Treatment
- Discuss the Client's Prior History of Compliance
- Discuss Current Compliance Problems Immediately
- Provide Aftercare Counseling Prior to Discharge from Residential or Inpatient Care
- Help the Client Anticipate Roadblocks to Change
- Encourage Discussions of the Counseling Process
- Encourage Discussions of the Client-Counselor Relationship
- Negotiate Rather Than Dictate Change Plans
- Emphasize the Client's Responsibility to Participate in Treatment
- Emphasize the Client's Responsibility to Change
- Provide Education to the Client and Family
- Provide Interventions Based on Empirical Support
- Elicit Family Support and Involvement
- Explore the Client's Expectations, Hopes, and Goals for Treatment
- Regularly Review Treatment Goals and Progress
- Discuss the Pros and Cons of Treatment and Self-Help Programs
- Discuss the Pros and Cons of Abstinence
- Provide Options Regarding Treatment
- Change Treatment Frequency and Intensity
- Provide Direct Feedback to Client
- Discuss the Client's Reactions to Feedback
- Provide Reinforcement for Treatment Compliance
- Address Anxiety about Treatment or Self-Help Group Attendance
- Monitor Substance-Abuse Recovery Issues
- Discuss Cravings and Thoughts of Using Substances
- Identify People, Places, Events, and Close Calls
- Assess Motivation to Change
- Monitor Substance-Use Relapse Warning Signs
- Monitor Psychiatric Symptoms
- Address Persistent or Residual Psychiatric Symptoms
- Monitor Psychiatric Relapse Warning Signs
- Consider the Use of Medications
- Prepare the Client for Taking Medications
- Monitor Medication Compliance
- Address Adverse Side Effects or Lack of Efficacy
- Facilitate Medication Changes for Ineffective Medicines
- Facilitate Augmentation Therapy
- Prepare for Negative Reactions from Self-Help Group Members to Medications

Chapter 6

Systems and Agency Strategies to Improve Compliance

Introduction

Treatment systems or agencies can implement policies, procedures, and strategies to improve client compliance. This chapter presents suggestions based on reports in the literature and our ongoing experience trying to improve ways in which we deliver clinical care in our treatment program.[1] While a particular agency or program should use strategies based on its capabilities and resources, most of the following suggestions can be widely implemented. (See chart 6, page 100 for a comprehensive list of systems strategies to improve compliance.)

Develop a Clinic Philosophy on Compliance

We believe each agency or treatment program should have a philosophy on how it understands and clinically approaches compliance problems, from treatment entry through early termination. Compliance-related problems are best viewed as clinical issues to be solved by the clinic rather than as reasons to negatively judge clients who struggle with their ability to comply with treatment. For example, most programs have an easily identifiable, high-risk group of clients who have the worst rates of compliance. Developing a philosophy on how to approach these high-risk clients benefits them as well as the counseling staff.

A clinical philosophy can emphasize the importance of continually attempting to engage clients in treatment rather than labeling poorly compliant clients as unmotivated, irresponsible, or in denial. The Motivational Enhancement Therapy model of treatment, for example, emphasizes that compliance problems belong to the clinician, not the client.[2] This model also emphasizes that it is the responsibility of the clinician to develop clinical interventions to address compliance problems.

Counselors often value the actual process of counseling much more than the "precounseling" stage. The counselor needs to accept that many clients will not be ready to change their substance use behaviors and may indeed be in the "precontemplation" or "contemplation" stage of change, and that focusing on "engagement" is just as important as focusing on "counseling" for these clients. (Please see chapter 7 for a discussion of these stages.)

A treatment system's philosophy should also include client education on motivation in recovery from substance use or dual disorders, stages of change, and common compliance problems. In a sense, providing client education on these issues is no different than providing education on the effects of alcohol or street drugs, medication side effects, or specific psychiatric disorders. The more clients understand an issue and the potential roadblocks associated with this issue (e.g., compliance), the more prepared they are to address it in ongoing recovery.

Encourage Staff Training on Motivational and Compliance Counseling

In recent years there has been an increase in clinical workshops, books, and materials on Motivational Interviewing, Motivational Enhancement Therapy, and Motivational Therapy.[3] Developed primarily by William Miller, Stephen Rollnick, and their colleagues, motivational approaches can be used with a variety of substance abuse disorders and dual disorders. We have successfully adapted motivational strategies for use with clients who have psychiatric disorders in addition to substance abuse disorders. We have used such strategies both to improve rates of compliance with outpatient treatment among recently discharged inpatients and to improve rates of compliance with scheduled outpatient treatment sessions. While chapters 7 through 10 provide more specific details on these interventions, suffice it to say that we're finding encouraging evidence that client-centered motivational interventions have a positive impact on clients and lead to improved compliance with treatment.

In our clinic, clinicians are well trained in several models of counseling including the traditional Twelve Step or Addiction Counseling model. We have found that clinicians can integrate client-centered motivational treatment approaches in their daily counseling while maintaining the integrity of current treatment models. We wish to emphasize that using motivational counseling strategies does not imply "giving up" one's old way of practicing clinical care. Rather, motivational approaches can be integrated within other treatment models.

Provide Early Access to Treatment

Early access to treatment is important in reducing barriers to following through with care. Many clients with substance use disorders are ambivalent about getting help and change their minds after making an appointment for evaluation. In a sense, clinics have to "strike while the iron is hot" and see clients as quickly as possible for their initial appointment. Clinics should keep spots open on the appointment calendar for scheduling new clients. The sooner a client is seen after making the initial telephone call for services, the greater the likelihood that he or she will show up for the evaluation. Waiting several days or longer substantially reduces compliance rates with the initial evaluation session. Clinics that have clients wait weeks or longer are likely to have even worse rates of compliance with the initial session. The first twenty-four hours after a client's initial call for help is a critical period in initiating treatment.[4]

Offer Flexible Appointment Times

Appointment times for evaluation and treatment sessions need to be flexible, particularly for clients who cannot take time off from work to attend. While residential rehabilitation or intensive outpatient programs often require the client to be absent from work, less intensive outpatient services need to offer day and evening sessions so that clients have maximum flexibility in getting counseling appointments. If a large portion of clinic clients works during the day, sufficient numbers of evening treatment slots or group sessions must be available to meet their clinical needs.

Offer Consistent Appointment Times

For clients who participate in ongoing individual or family treatment sessions, keeping the day and time of appointment the same makes it easier for clients to remember appointment times and get in the habit of attending. This also helps reduce the possibility of other events interfering with the client's keeping the scheduled appointment. If clients know that their weekly or biweekly counseling appointments are on Tuesdays at 4:00 P.M., they can schedule other commitments and activities at a different time.

Call and Remind Clients of the Initial Evaluation Session

Many studies and clinical experience show that far too many clients with alcohol or other drug problems fail to show up for, and reschedule, their initial evaluation. A friendly telephone call by the assessing clinician or the program's secretary can improve the rates of compliance. In our dual diagnosis and substance abuse treatment program, we find that a telephone call reminding the client about the appointment increases the appearance rate by about 15 percent. This reminder is best made a day or two before the scheduled appointment.

Call Clients Who Fail to Show Up for the Initial Evaluation

A friendly telephone call can be made to individuals who fail to show up for or cancel their initial evaluation. While some will refuse another appointment, others will appreciate the gesture and keep their rescheduled appointment. If individuals refuse another appointment time, the clinic can encourage them to call back should they later decide to follow through with the evaluation. This message conveys respect for the client's decision while leaving the door open for him or her to enter treatment.

Clients who do not have telephones can be sent a "user-friendly" letter, either with another appointment time or with instructions to call the clinic to reschedule their evaluation. Giving another appointment time in the letter eliminates the need for the client to call the clinic. However, an appointment slot is taken that could be used for another client. Another variation is to offer a new evaluation time and ask the client to call the counselor to verify the appointment.

Call Clients or Family Members Prior to Regularly Scheduled Treatment Sessions

Some treatment programs routinely call all clients or families prior to their scheduled individual or group sessions, a practice commonly used by dentists and other health care professionals as well. In one of the mental health clinics in our medical center, the secretary called with a reminder one day prior to the individual therapy appointment or group treatment session. This practice increased compliance rates by 10 to 15 percent.

For clinics with limited resources, there are several variations of this procedure. One is to call only new clients during the first several weeks of counseling until they get used to coming in for sessions. Another is to call only those clients identified as high-risk for compliance based on prior experience in treatment or current level of motivation. Using client or family volunteers to make reminder calls is another variation. If this procedure is used, due to confidentiality issues, the clinic must get written, informed consent from clients so that they can be called by a volunteer. In a family program conducted for clients in residential treatment, we used family members participating in aftercare family groups to call new family members two days prior to the scheduled weekend program. Family attendance more than doubled and we believe that this procedure played a significant role in improving family compliance.

Use Prompts to Remind Clients of Scheduled Sessions

How many counselors have forgotten about dentist, doctor, or other appointments because they didn't write down the day and time? Appointment cards are excellent reminders to clients of scheduled sessions. These can be carried in wallets or purses or put in a prominent place in the home such as on the refrigerator or bulletin board. Clients can also use calendars to keep track of appointments at the clinic, other appointments, and even self-help group meetings. Counselors can encourage clients to review their calendars daily as a reminder of treatment and self-help activities. In cases of partial hospital or intensive outpatient programs, counselors can provide clients with a schedule of daily, weekly, and monthly treatment sessions and activities.

Use Written Compliance Contracts

For clients with histories of poor compliance or current compliance problems, the clinic can develop a template for a written compliance contract. The contract should provide space to state the problem, the solution, client responsibilities, and the consequences of breaking the contract. A written contract is a concrete reminder to the client of the importance of following the treatment plan.

Use Creative Ways of Scheduling Treatment Appointments

Missed treatment appointments not only risk endangering a client's recovery but also represent lost revenue for the agency. Counselors can use a variety of creative ways to limit "lost" clinical hours. One way is to have clinicians use three-hour blocks of time in which four individual counseling sessions can be scheduled, each for forty-five minutes. Since most payers consider forty-five to fifty minutes as a full counseling session, this strategy reduces the likelihood of the clinic's losing income due to missed appointments because three hours worth of revenues can be gained even when 25 percent of clients miss their scheduled counseling sessions. In addition, when a session is missed, the counselor can use the time to call noncompliant clients, complete paperwork, or focus on other tasks.

Another strategy to reduce lost clinical time is to schedule brief sessions (twenty-five to thirty minutes) for poorly compliant clients who agree to return for sessions. After they attend an agreed-on number of brief sessions, they can be given longer counseling appointments.

Finally, clients who continue to miss individual appointments, despite the counselor's attempts to change this behavior, can be required to attend a set number of group sessions before an individual appointment is given. For example, in our clinic, we sometimes ask clients who repeatedly miss individual sessions to attend two to four stabilization group sessions before they are given individual counseling appointments.

Provide Outreach to Poorly Compliant Clients

The most poorly compliant clients are often the most likely to suffer severe consequences when they do not comply with treatment. These clients can take a great deal of the counselor's time and energy, especially in times of crisis. One strategy to address this group of clients is to have an aggressive outreach philosophy and plan. Clinics can reach out in a variety of ways, including using friendly telephone calls or letters to invite clients to return to treatment, using motivational strategies to attempt to persuade them to return to treatment, offering brief telephone sessions to buy the client time before deciding whether or not to return to treatment, or making home visits. Clinics can also use recovering volunteers or case managers for these outreach activities.

Encourage Treatment Dropouts to Return for Services

In discussions with treatment dropouts, counselors can encourage them to return for services. They should convey the message that it is never too late to change or benefit from treatment, regardless of what occurred previously. This requires a nonjudgmental attitude and an ability to convey hope rather than mistrust to the client. Counselors need to keep in mind that many people with substance use disorders often make numerous attempts at getting help before they ultimately succeed.[5]

Determine the Reasons for Poor Compliance or Early Treatment Dropout

Interviews or questionnaires can be used to discover reasons for poor treatment compliance or early treatment dropout in prior episodes of care. The counselor can simply ask clients to identify reasons. Or, the counselor can prompt clients by reviewing a list of common reasons and ask them to identify which reasons they believe contribute to their problems with compliance (e.g., reasons such as relocating; difficulties with transportation or child care; medical problems; not liking treatment, the treatment clinic atmosphere, or the counselor; being angry at treatment staff for tardiness in starting sessions).

Clients often are able to identify multiple reasons for poor compliance or early treatment termination. The counselor can ask them to rank their reasons, beginning with the most influential. This information can help the client use past decisions as a learning experience and develop a plan to reduce the probability of poor compliance during the current course of treatment. This process is similar to identifying factors that may have contributed to a relapse, thus turning a negative event into an educational one. In such a review, counselors sometimes discover that clinic- or systems-related problems contributed to compliance problems.

Use Case Management Services

Clients with substance use or dual disorders frequently experience many life problems. They often need help accessing a range of other services or programs. Case management (CM) services can help clients with these problems. While CM services have traditionally been used more frequently in treatment programs for the chronically mentally ill, in recent years these services have played an increasingly valuable role in the treatment of substance use disorders.[6] CM includes a variety of functions such as assessing other service needs (medical, economic, legal, housing, vocational, etc.), accessing services that can address these needs, removing barriers that prevent the client from using other services, monitoring compliance with other services, providing outreach to poorly compliant clients to reengage them in services, advocating on behalf of clients, teaching practical life skills (e.g., finding an apartment, shopping for food, budgeting), and helping with problem-solving and crisis intervention. One study found that 90 percent of IV-drug-abusing clients who received CM services entered substance abuse treatment; among those who did not receive CM services only 35 percent entered treatment.[7]

Help the Client Access Other Services

Alcohol and drug abuse counselors who lack the aid of case managers can facilitate their clients' use of other services or help them solve problems that are likely to interfere with treatment. For example, in our clinic many clients need help locating public housing or long-term community residential programs, applying for public welfare benefits (medical care, food stamps, financial aid), or applying for vocational assessment, counseling, or training services. In addition, a good number of our clients need help dealing with their children's mental health problems. This often requires facilitating a referral to a program for children and adolescents. Cases involving the use of other programs require collaboration between the counselor and those involved in providing services to clients. The counselor can also help the client anticipate roadblocks or barriers that might get in the way of the client following through with a referral. Strategies can be discussed so that the client is more likely to comply with the referral to another service.

Contact Client to Make Sure Referrals Were Followed Up

If a client is referred to another agency or service, the counselor can call to find out if the client kept the appointment. If not, the counselor can contact the client by phone to discuss the client's current status and needs and encourage him or her to follow through with the referral. If the client cannot be reached by phone, the counselor can write a brief, user-friendly letter encouraging the client to contact the agency or to call the counselor to discuss any questions or concerns.

Provide Assistance with Practical Problems

Problems with child care and transportation often interfere with a client's ability to comply with scheduled treatment sessions and can be a major factor in dropping out of treatment early. Some strategies include facilitating the client's purchase of discounted bus passes, providing free bus tickets for low-income clients, and providing child care on the clinic's premises. The clinic can help with other practical problems that impact compliance. For example, Brad, a young man with a limited income, was instructed to take his medications with food in order to reduce the chances of nausea. His limited income meant that he sometimes had little food to eat. As a result, he did not take his medicine. Helping Brad use community resources, such as a food bank, kept him from going hungry and missing medication doses.

Establish Clinic and Counselor Thresholds for Acceptable Levels of Treatment Compliance or Completion

A clinic can elicit input from counseling and supervisory staff to determine acceptable levels of treatment compliance or completion. Advantages of establishing these thresholds include having clear-cut benchmarks for the staff to meet as a group and as individual clinicians, identifying potential problems early (e.g., when a counselor's or the clinic's compliance rates are below the accepted thresholds), and providing a gauge to measure the clinic's viability as a business. Many clinics operate on fee-for-service schedules and only get reimbursed for work actually done with clients. Missed sessions therefore lead to loss of income and can threaten the survival of the clinic. Counselors who do not meet thresholds can be helped to develop a plan to improve compliance rates. Counselors who exceed the thresholds can be rewarded if possible (e.g., by letters of commendation, higher levels of annual salary increments, support to attend conferences). Client compliance rates with scheduled counseling sessions can be a regular part of the job evaluations of clinicians.

Conduct Regular Client and Family Satisfaction Surveys

Satisfaction surveys can be conducted at regular intervals (e.g., every three months) or at the end of each client's treatment. These surveys allow clients and families to rate quality of services received, degree to which their needs were met by the treatment provided, level of satisfaction with services, and whether or not they would recommend the program to a friend in need, or return in the future if they needed help again. Surveys can also help a clinic find out what clients and families liked best or least about its services. Information gained from satisfaction surveys can be used to improve services.

Continuously Seek Quality Improvement

While some review agencies mandate quality assurance and quality improvement measures, it is a good idea for a clinic to always look for ways to improve its services as these may have a positive impact on compliance rates. A simple process to follow is:

- *Ask staff or clients to identify problems or concerns related to the problems treated in the clinic* (e.g., lateness for treatment groups, poor attendance at self-help group meetings, low rates of family involvement in sessions, poor rates of show for the initial outpatient appointment for discharged inpatients, poor compliance with medication, early termination from treatment).

- *Attempt to quantify the problem identified* (e.g., 25 percent of clients are regularly late for group sessions, only 45 percent of clients utilize self-help groups in the community, only 38 percent of discharged inpatients show for the initial outpatient appointment).
- *Identify an acceptable level related to the problem identified* (e.g., less than 10 percent of clients will be late for group sessions, more than 70 percent of clients will participate in community self-help groups, 65 percent of discharged inpatients will show for their initial outpatient appointment).
- *Identify one or more specific interventions to impact on the problem identified* (e.g., clients will be oriented to groups and the importance of being on time as they are only allowed to enter group within the first five minutes of the start of the group session; clients will be oriented to self-help groups in the community and another recovering person will offer to accompany them to meetings; each inpatient will receive a single motivational counseling session by an outpatient clinician prior to discharge from the hospital).
- *Identify how change will be measured* (e.g., group leaders will record on the sign-in sheet any client who is more than five minutes late for the group session; counselors will record self-help group attendance for all clients; rates of compliance with the initial outpatient session for discharged inpatients will be recorded for all referrals and reported to the program director on a weekly basis; the program director will keep ongoing statistics on the number of clients who show for their initial outpatient appointment).
- *Compare pre- and postintervention data to determine if it has had any impact on the problem identified* (e.g., lateness for group sessions has decreased by 18

percent, 68 percent of clients have attended self-help meetings, and 72 percent of inpatients referred to the outpatient clinic have appeared for their initial appointment following hospital discharge).

- *Write up and communicate results.* If results are negative or neutral, then the clinic should consider other interventions to address the problem. If results are positive and maintained over a period of time, the clinic can use the interventions as a usual part of clinic care and then identify new problem areas to address. Counselors can share positive results with peers in other clinics or in private practice.

Offer Integrated Treatment for Clients with Dual Disorders

There are three general paradigms for the treatment of clients with both substance use and psychiatric disorders: parallel, sequential, and integrated.[8] *Parallel treatment* involves the client receiving mental health services and substance abuse services in separate programs or agencies at the same time. *Sequential treatment* involves the client stabilizing on one disorder first, then seeking treatment for the other disorder. In this paradigm, one client may first receive mental health services, then substance abuse services while another may receive services in the reverse order. This model assumes the most prominent disorder is treated first. *Integrated treatment* involves focusing on both mental health and substance abuse issues simultaneously in the same treatment program.[9]

Several recent studies and papers provide evidence that the integrated approach is more effective than the parallel or sequential approaches, particularly among clients with more chronic and persistent forms of mental illness.[10] Offering integrated treatment services or referring more severely ill dual diagnosis clients to integrated programs is likely to be more

Chart 6
Systems Strategies to Improve Compliance

- Develop a Clinic Philosophy on Compliance
- Encourage Staff Training on Motivational and Compliance Counseling
- Provide Early Access to Treatment
- Offer Flexible Appointment Times
- Offer Consistent Appointment Times
- Call and Remind Clients of the Initial Evaluation Session
- Call Clients Who Fail to Show Up for the Initial Evaluation
- Call Clients or Family Members Prior to Regularly Scheduled Treatment Sessions
- Use Prompts to Remind Clients of Scheduled Sessions
- Use Written Compliance Contracts
- Use Creative Ways of Scheduling Treatment Appointments
- Provide Outreach to Poorly Compliant Clients
- Encourage Treatment Dropouts to Return for Services
- Determine the Reasons for Poor Compliance or Early Treatment Dropout
- Use Case Management Services
- Help the Client Access Other Services
- Contact Client to Make Sure Referrals Were Followed Up
- Provide Assistance with Practical Problems
- Establish Clinic and Counselor Thresholds for Acceptable Levels of Treatment Compliance or Completion
- Conduct Regular Client and Family Satisfaction Surveys
- Continuously Seek Quality Improvement
- Offer Integrated Treatment for Clients with Dual Disorders

effective for this difficult subgroup of clients. We have observed that many mental health and substance abuse treatment programs are offering dual diagnosis services. While some programs ensure that staff are appropriately trained and offer true dual diagnosis services, the staff of other programs are less well trained and less able to take adequate care of clients with dual disorders. It's one thing to offer traditional substance abuse outpatient services to a high-functioning client with a depressive disorder who is stable on antidepressant medications. Treatment in this case can focus primarily on the alcohol or other drug problem, especially if the symptoms of depression are in remission or relatively mild in nature. However, it's another thing to offer traditional substance abuse outpatient services to a client with chronic schizophrenia or bipolar disorder who has had multiple psychiatric hospitalizations. Treatment is likely to fail if sufficient attention is not directed to the symptoms and problems of the mental disorder.

PART three

Clinical Applications of Motivational Strategies

Chapter 7

A Motivational Approach to Improving Compliance

Introduction

In the preceding chapters we have described strategies that can be used by counselors to improve clients' compliance with treatment. The advantage of access to such a range of useful interventions is the relative ease with which counselors may find those that fit both the necessities of the moment and the specifics of their individual styles and situations.

In this, the book's final section, we will present an integrated approach for improving compliance that incorporates many of the strategies already described. This approach improves the compliance of clients by targeting the specific issue of clients' motivation for treatment and change—their willingness to engage in the difficult process of exploring their own contributions to their problems and deciding how to change with the assistance of helping professionals.

The premise of our approach is simple: counselors will be most successful in retaining clients if those clients want what the counselor has to offer. In this chapter, we will introduce the general approach, describing and illustrating its basic concepts. In the chapters that follow, we will show how the model can be applied at points along the spectrum of the treatment engagement process—from the initial phone call from a person seeking help with a substance abuse problem (chapter 8), to the transition from inpatient or residential treatment to aftercare (chapter 9), to the initial sessions of an outpatient treatment episode (chapter 10).

Taken as a whole, this section requires a significant shift in thinking where client participation in treatment is concerned. It therefore asks counselors to be willing to view familiar situations anew. If this bears a striking similarity to what counselors ask of their clients, the resemblance is more than coincidental.

Understanding Resistance

1. Think of an important decision you've been trying to make—one that's hanging over your head right now. Choose a situation that really matters to you. Now answer this question: for how long have you been trying to make this decision?
2. Imagine that you must decide, right now, what you are going to do. Your decision must be definite and permanent; not only must you stick to it, but also you must actively work to realize it. And, no matter how hard the decision is or how many obstacles you encounter in carrying it out, you may not have any second thoughts about it; uncertainty will be judged as evidence that you are not serious about your decision or that you are planning to go back on it, in direct violation of the agreement.

We have conducted this exercise with counselors in numerous workshops over the past few years, and it has produced remarkably consistent results. Participants report thinking of major life decisions in a wide range of areas: change jobs or stay where I am? move to a new city or stay put? go back to school or keep working with my current degree? marry this person or not? quit smoking, go on a diet, or just go with the flow? But as diverse as these situations are, the decisions are almost always ones that the participants have been considering not for days, or even weeks, but for months or even years—in fact, twenty-five years is the "record" so far.

When we tell participants to choose *now,* the vast majority communicate the message that they'll do no such thing:

- "You can't make us do that! What right do you have? . . ."
- [Silent, arms folded, looking away]
- "You don't understand—I don't like my job anymore, but things are really tight in the field right now, and I don't know whether I'll be able to get something else or . . ."
- [Worried expression, edging up on seat, looking for the door]
- "Sure, whatever you say. . . ."

Whether angry and argumentative, quiet and sullen, rationalizing and excuse-making, anxious and avoidant, or pseudocooperative, these reactions demonstrate that the *best way to generate resistance to change is to insist on change.* In fact, the stronger the pressure, the more participants dig in against it.

But why should this be? After all, isn't it the job of workshop leaders—as experts in the area of promoting change—to tell participants what to do and how to do it?

There are two kinds of answers to this question.

1. Whatever the leaders' credentials or claims to expertise, they are unknown quantities to their clients—their values, assumptions, and ways of dealing with problems are all unfamiliar. Similarly, their trustworthiness and commitment to the best interests of others remain unproven.
2. The leaders' understanding of the specific problem

> and all the considerations that must go into the decision is limited. Difficult and important decisions leave people feeling torn and anxious. Much is riding on making the "right" choice, and the "wrong" one may result in painful feelings of regret, self-doubt, and even shame (not to mention a hated job or an undesired spouse). To make such a decision precipitously, at someone else's insistence, would only intensify that anxiety.

For most participants, these two factors are powerful obstacles to cooperation, much less acquiescence. Yet at least one participant almost always responds by saying, "Fine! I'll choose _____." In some cases, this is just a variation on the "pseudocooperative" response—going along outwardly without any real intention of acting on what's been agreed on. But sometimes, the person really seems to entertain the possibility of deciding once and for all. How is this sudden decisiveness after months or years of uncertainty to be understood?

A useful comparison might be with an encounter with a "hard-sell" salesperson. Many people walk into auto dealerships or electronics stores with the intention of just looking around and seeing what their options are, but find themselves walking out having signed a contract for a new car or big-screen TV. How did this happen? Usually they've run into a salesperson who, with a combination of charm, fast talk, and answers for every objection, has corralled them into a decision they hadn't been ready to make.

Some of these buyers are relieved. They really wanted that car or TV but either were afraid to make a commitment or knew in their hearts that they couldn't quite afford what they wanted. The salesperson gave them the push they needed, that is, the push they *wanted* but couldn't quite give themselves. These people have been given the gift of *freedom from choice*. In the whirlwind of the purchase, they can rely on the salesperson's enthusiasm to reassure them that they've made the right decision and, if they later have regrets, the salesperson can take the rap and spare them the unpleasant recognition that they made the wrong one.

On the other hand, some impulse buyers start to have second thoughts from the moment they leave the store: "What was I thinking? How am I going to pay for this? Do I really even want a new car?" Plagued with "buyer's remorse," they soon look for ways to undo what they've done.

People who are close to a major decision, but feel afraid to take the risk, may well be "convinced" by a firm push. (Of course, a gentler push might be just as effective in many cases.) Some of these people will forge ahead, relieved. Others regret their hastiness and, unprepared for the new reality they've committed themselves to, will soon renege on the deal, settling back into more-or-less tortured indecision and resentment of the person who almost "made" them decide before they were ready. Still others, having given verbal assent to whatever demands have been made upon them, will remain pleasant and cooperative until they are no longer within range of the source of the pressure—and then go blithely on as before, no closer to a real decision. And this accounting does not even include the many who, openly put off by the pushiness of the "hard sell," will stiffen their resolve to resist any efforts to convince them.

The implications for the counselor working with substance-abusing or dual-disordered clients are clear: what is typically thought of as "resistance" is often the completely normal tendency of human beings to protect their own sense of independence and freedom to choose in their own time. If counselors are to engage clients in treatment during the earliest part of their recoveries—when they are most uncertain about the decision to get and stay clean and sober, and anxious about trying to get through the day without using substances—then they must avoid creating or intensifying clients' resistance.

Many counselors are amazed at how much easier their work becomes when they stop insisting that their clients make a change, right now, because they (as "experts" in addictive behavior) believe that the time is right and that it's in the client's best interest to do so. One workshop participant said that after years of confronting clients, he got tired of hitting his head against a brick wall and coming away bloody—which recalls the old joke:

Patient: "Doctor, it hurts when I lift my arm like this."
Doctor: "Then don't lift your arm like this!"

Yet despite many counselors' occasional awareness of how frustrating it can be to go on working in a style that may lead to arguments, tension, and even painfully unproductive interactions, their good intentions are often their worst enemies: out of the wish to be helpful and to positively influence the client comes the dreaded encounter with their nemesis, the "unmotivated" client.

"There's a Hole in My Bucket": Creating an "Unmotivated" Client

The traditional children's song "There's a Hole in My Bucket" provides a useful illustration of the phenomenon of creating an unmotivated client. The song is a conversation between Henry, who has the problem named in the title, and Liza, the practical-minded girl Henry addresses and who takes his initial statement as a request for advice.

There's a hole in my bucket, dear Liza, dear Liza,
There's a hole in my bucket, dear Liza, a hole.

Then mend it, dear Henry, dear Henry, dear Henry,
Then mend it, dear Henry, dear Henry, mend it.

The lyrics of this song mimic a certain kind of counseling dialogue: the client (Henry) describes what sounds to the counselor (Liza) like a clearly defined problem, and the counselor attempts to set the tone for what is to follow by conveying that it is the client who will have to do the work of solving it. The client, however, seems to have another idea.

With what shall I mend it, dear Liza, dear Liza,
With what shall I mend it, dear Liza, with what?

In asking for advice, the client counters the counselor's message with another: if you want me to solve my problem, you're going to have to tell me how. In essence, the client insists that, if the counselor is going to set herself up as someone who helps to solve problems, but isn't actually going to solve his problem for him, then the least the counselor should do is to tell him how to solve it for himself. Sounds reasonable enough—and so the counselor attempts to do so.

With some straw, dear Henry, dear Henry, dear Henry,
With some straw, dear Henry, dear Henry, some straw.

Now the counselor has made it clear that she is an expert in the particular area of bucket holes and that she will provide the client with the information he needs to solve his problem. Naturally, the client has questions about how exactly this all works.

The straw is too long, dear Liza, dear Liza,
The straw is too long, dear Liza, too long.

Then cut it, dear Henry, dear Henry, dear Henry,
Then cut it, dear Henry, dear Henry, then cut it.
With what shall I cut it, dear Liza, dear Liza,
With what shall I cut it, dear Liza, with what?

Uh-oh. The counselor has probably begun to realize that the more advice she offers, the more questions the client asks. She may be beginning to suspect that the client is asking questions *instead* of trying to solve the problem. Or, she may simply be beginning to feel that the client just isn't trying very hard.

With a knife, dear Henry, dear Henry, dear Henry,
With a knife, dear Henry, dear Henry, with a knife.
The knife is too dull, dear Liza, dear Liza,
The knife is too dull, dear Liza, too dull.
Then sharpen it, dear Henry, dear Henry, dear Henry,
Then sharpen it, dear Henry, dear Henry, sharpen it.
With what shall I sharpen it, dear Liza, dear Liza,
With what shall I sharpen it, dear Liza, with what?

By this point it is clear to all except Henry—and perhaps to Henry too—that things have taken a rather unhelpful turn somewhere along the way. Indeed, in one popular rendition[1] Liza's growing exasperation with Henry comes across in her tone of voice and in the sighs that punctuate her responses.

As the song wends its way painfully to its end, Liza begins to moan each time her answer begets yet another question.

With a stone, dear Henry, dear Henry, dear Henry,
With a stone, dear Henry, dear Henry, with a stone.
The stone is too dry, dear Liza, dear Liza,
The stone is too dry, dear Liza, too dry.
Then wet it, dear Henry, dear Henry, dear Henry,
Then wet it, dear Henry, dear Henry, then wet it.

With what shall I wet it, dear Liza, dear Liza,
With what shall I wet it, dear Liza, with what?
With water, dear Henry, dear Henry, dear Henry,
With water, dear Henry, dear Henry, with water.
In what shall I get it, dear Liza, dear Liza,
In what shall I get it, dear Liza, in what?

With dawning horror, the listeners anticipate the song's inevitable conclusion. Liza, too, seems to see what's coming; yet she is powerless to stop it, trapped as she is in the dialogical structure she has participated in creating.

In a bucket, dear Henry, dear Henry, dear Henry,
In a bucket, dear Henry, dear Henry, in a bucket.
There's a hole in my bucket, dear Liza, dear Liza,
There's a hole in my bucket, dear Liza, a hole.

With this, Liza lets out a shriek, and the song comes crashing to its end. Three things seem unmistakable: that this enterprise has been an exercise in futility; that Liza will dread any future installment of it; and that Henry has certainly not been given much reason to come back and continue the discussion.

Resistance and the Unmotivated Client

What lessons can be drawn from this old song? Like Henry, some clients appear to resist every intervention while acting as though they want help. These are surely among the most frustrating people with whom counselors work.

Liza's transparent lack of genuineness—demonstrated by her continuing to address her inquisitor as "dear" when he is clearly anything *but* dear to her at that moment—exemplifies how counselors may deny their own anger and frustration toward such a client. This creates further complications: the client cannot help but become aware of the counselor's suppressed feelings, which inevitably leak through in tone of voice, exasperated sighs, and general impatience; the client is then likely to begin both to mistrust the counselor and to internalize the message that real feelings are too risky to express directly.

But even more fundamental than these considerations is the issue of how counselors come to see a client either as too lazy, foolish, or dependent to use their good offerings, or, more likely, as "unmotivated"—a word they may also use to justify giving up on clients who have frustrated counselors' best efforts to help them. "There's a Hole in My Bucket" is usually understood as the story of a young man unable to solve or think through his own problem despite the heroic efforts of his female friend and advisor, who is finally trapped by the young man's obtuse helplessness. We would suggest the opposite: Henry's ever-increasing helplessness is a direct response to Liza's eagerness to tell him what to do, and a remarkably effective way of defeating it.

When clients are overwhelmed by a problem that they unambivalently wish to solve, they generally greet efforts to help them with receptiveness and gratitude. Though Henry initially gives the appearance of being such a client, it is not long before he begins systematically to undermine Liza's efforts. His questions become increasingly absurd, reaching their lowest point with the stupefying "With what shall I wet it?"

To see Henry as so cognitively or emotionally limited as to need to be told to mend something he already knew to be broken is to condescend to him, whatever Liza's good intentions. Failing to consider that Henry might not be telling her about his bucket problem in order to get advice, but for some other reason, she leaps immediately into the mode of "fixer" and helps to create the nightmarish scenario in which she inextricably finds herself. Frustrated and bewildered, she does not recognize in his neediness an exaggerated version of the role she has prepared for him: the passive, obedient child who must be told exactly what to do from start to finish and cannot be expected to think for himself or act on his own.

Of course, the passively resistant Henry is only one of many versions of the unmotivated client. Another Henry might immediately demand that Liza fix the bucket for him, or at least help to get him a new one; yet another might insist that the bucket is *fine* with a hole in it or that the hole is so small that it hardly matters and certainly isn't worth trying to fix. Liza might then insist that she can see very clearly that there's a hole, that the leak is serious and creating all kinds of problems, and that if Henry can't see this then he must be blind or self-deceived. An argument would ensue, most likely resulting in frayed tempers and a bucket that still leaks.

In each case Liza assumes that Henry wants and expects to be told what to do and that her job is to tell him. "There's a Hole in My Bucket" and its variants thus provide an excellent illustration of what can happen when a counselor tries to offer advice, education, or direction to a client whose wishes and motivations regarding their work together are unclear, and whose feelings about "solving the problem" have not been explored.

Any number of preliminary issues that have not been raised and questions that remain unanswered might have laid the groundwork for a more successful outcome to Henry and Liza's discussion. What is Henry's view of the problem? Why is he telling Liza about the problem? Does he even see the situation *as* a problem? If so, how does he feel about trying to solve the problem? And is he truly interested in being helped to solve the problem?

Here is an alternate scenario to consider: instead of imposing her own ideas and approach and then wondering why

Henry fails to act on them, what if Liza tried to draw out Henry's own expertise and ideas about how to solve the problem or to deal with the situation, or inquired about what kinds of approaches seemed workable to him? She might find that his uncertainties about how to proceed mask uncertainty about *whether* to proceed. She might consider the possibility that he may have reasons for *not* wanting to fix that damn hole or fears about what may happen if he tries and fails—or tries and *succeeds*. And she might recognize the necessity of exploring and resolving these sources of hesitation before moving on to the question of how to "fix" things.

Obviously, we are talking here about much more than fixing bucket holes, and our illustration may itself be in danger of springing a leak from overwork. We are talking about how "resistance" and "lack of motivation," typically attributed by counselors to their clients alone, may in fact be exacerbated by counselors' ignoring or trying to forcibly overcome clients' complex mixture of thoughts and feelings about counseling and change. This idea has important implications for attempts to intervene around the issues of motivation for change and treatment participation.

Lowering Resistance and Improving Compliance

We have successfully applied this perspective on motivation to our work with substance-abusing and dual-disordered clients, and we will present our interventions in detail in the following chapters of this book. Though they differ according to the specific needs of the situation they were designed to improve, each orients the counselor toward trying to arrive at a shared sense of what clients want and how ready they are to receive it. In creating this mutual understanding, the counselor is often helping as well to create in clients the willingness to attempt significant life change and the belief that they are able to succeed at it.

Our approach draws heavily on Motivational Interviewing. This counseling method was pioneered by the psychologists William Miller and Stephen Rollnick, and its success in increasing clients' motivation for change has been well documented.[2] Rather than understand motivation as a stable trait immune to influence, this approach views motivation as especially sensitive to interactions with others, especially those persons in whom an individual is in some way emotionally invested. Adapting this approach via Dennis Daley and Michael Thase's model of Dual Disorders Recovery Counseling,[3] we designed interventions to help clients to articulate their own concerns and to move of their own volition toward change.

Addressing the client in a primarily empathic and collaborative manner is central to our approach. We believe that this approach is more likely to increase motivation and compliance than either the more traditional "confrontational," or authoritarian, stance or more recently developed approaches that attempt to address client problems through immediate and direct education and guidance. The motivational perspective sees efforts by counselors to smash through walls of client "denial" as tending to create a dynamic of domination and submission, which is more likely to drive clients away or stiffen resistance to change than to facilitate compliance. Attempts to train clients in recovery skills from the very first contact, on the other hand, are judged from the motivational perspective to miss a crucial opportunity: the chance to engage clients in an active process of mobilizing their own resources and finding their own solutions.

Rather than telling clients from the start what to do or

what is right, then, the motivational counselor seeks first to understand clients' perspectives and to highlight their untapped strengths. This approach allows counselors to help clients find their own, individualized ways through the morass of fear and suffering created or exacerbated by their substance abuse.

Motivation becomes the focus of intervention because substance-abusing and dual-disordered clients are confused and afraid, regardless of the mask of indifference or hostility they may hide behind. Most are profoundly ambivalent about their behavior and the need for change. While painfully aware of the havoc their substance abuse is wreaking in their lives, they are at the same time deeply attached to their way of living and coping with problems and stresses. The motivational counselor views this ambivalence not as a form of pathological denial unique to substance-abusing persons but as a normal part of the *change process*, which typically involves passing through phases of obliviousness ("precontemplation"), ambivalence ("contemplation"), and resolution ("preparation") before action is taken and then maintained.[4]

Substance-abusing and dual-disordered clients, who often have limited experience following through with a plan of action or seeing their efforts succeed, may also have powerful incentive *not* to clearly recognize the need for changes that require commitment, consistency, tenacity, willingness to work, and tolerance for the frustration inherent in learning any new idea or skill. Their low sense of *self-efficacy*[5] tends to make any such attempts seem futile and defeating; they thus feel little inclination to face a reality that requires them to accept a stigmatized identity (alcoholic/addict), which they believe they have little hope of escaping. (This may be doubly true for dual-disordered clients, who are asked to accept what may be the two most stigmatizing labels society has to offer: addict and mental patient.) Instead, they may protect whatever fragile sense of self they possess by directing their energies toward survival and deflection of blame.

Whatever the counselor's "objective" assessment of their clients' situations might be, only their clients' *problem acceptance*—their subjective willingness to recognize the seriousness of the problem and the consequences of their behavior, as well as the need for action—is relevant to increasing motivation and readiness to change. But this then raises a second form of ambivalence, which also affects motivation: doubts clients have about the extent to which they can rely on their counselors to respect their autonomy while offering support and assistance.

Many substance-abusing and dual-disordered clients have come to expect—from experiences with dysfunctional parents, overburdened teachers, impatient juvenile justice systems—that those with power or influence over them are likely to respond in one of three ways: authoritarian, exploitative, or uncaring. The first of these may take the form of control, criticism, blame, punishment, attack; the second may involve manipulation, intrusion, or advantage-taking; the third might come across in misunderstanding, incompetence, neglect, insincerity, devaluation. In each case, these forms of betrayal or violation leave these individuals wary of depending on anyone to help them with their troubles.

Lacking the implicit sense of hopeful expectation, positive valuation, or instrumental orientation toward treatment that psychoanalysts refer to as "unobjectionable positive transference" or "basic trust,"[6] yet desperate for warmth and understanding, substance-abusing and dual-disordered clients often form "hostile-dependent" relationships with anyone who offers help, devaluing what has been offered while at the same time demanding assistance.[7] Developing the client's *treatment acceptance*—the willingness to genuinely engage in a helping relationship, instead of either openly defying or emptily complying with the helper—will require the counselor to avoid reenacting with the client the very kind of interactions the client both dreads and expects.

Motivational Strategies for Improving Compliance

Improving treatment compliance requires more than avoiding interactions that raise resistance, important as this may be. What positive qualities and approaches can lead clients to trust their counselors enough to accept help in taking a new step or making a difficult decision in the face of uncertainty?

Perhaps the best way to answer this question is with a clinical example.

- Although Joyce, age thirty-nine, had a long history of alcohol dependence, she had been sober for several months. Joyce had a high school education but had stayed home to raise her young son. Her husband held a good job and was generally reliable, except when, at least two to three times a year, he would go on a bender that might last as long as two weeks. In the past, Joyce had participated in many of these binges. Now sober and in counseling, she had begun to express some anxiety about what might happen when the next one came and she refused to join in.

  The answer came soon enough: Joyce came to a session one day wearing a large pair of dark glasses, beneath which was an ugly black eye. Her counselor immediately went into a crisis-response mode. He emphasized the need to ensure her safety, proposing options for her to get out of the house with her son, naming various shelters, warning her that her husband would no doubt express remorse when he sobered up but that clinical experience proved (especially in light of the counselor's knowledge that this was not the first time her husband had become violent when drinking) that he would likely hit her again in the future.

Joyce's responses were striking and consistent. Each time her counselor made a point about the danger of the situation, or suggested a way for her to ensure her safety, she replied with a reason why she could not possibly leave. She had not worked in many years and had no idea how she would support herself; her son loved his school and would be devastated if he had to change it; all her possessions were in the house and there would be no way to get them out without her husband knowing about it, which would prompt him to destroy everything or attack her again.

Joyce's counselor became acutely aware that they were getting nowhere and that he was becoming frustrated and impatient. He was beginning to see the whole discussion as pointless and was wondering what was wrong with Joyce's judgment when a lightbulb went off in his head. He then continued: *You know, Joyce, as I think about the things you've been telling me, all of the problems with leaving the situation you're in, it sounds to me like the decision that makes the most sense is just for you to stay where you are.* Joyce fixed the counselor with an unblinking stare, and replied: *What are you, crazy?* She then went on to tell the counselor all the reasons why she ought to get herself out of there: she'd worked before and she could work again; she'd miss her stuff but that meant a whole lot less than putting up with getting hit again; going to a shelter would be hard to take, but it wouldn't be permanent, and she'd been through

> worse; her son would be hurt a lot more by seeing his dad beat his mom than by changing schools. . . .

Once Joyce's counselor stopped trying to persuade her to do what he thought she should do, but instead tried to understand how she was seeing her situation, Joyce no longer had to defend her autonomy. She also could see that the counselor *did* understand her, or at least that he understood her *fears*, and that she did not have to worry about his minimizing the difficulty of the choice she was facing. Instead, she was free to look at the image in the mirror the counselor was holding up to her and to recognize that it was distorted, that it reflected *only* her fears, but not her strengths or her values or her hopes for herself and her son. And having recognized this, she could lay out in no uncertain terms the other side of the story—the one that was hidden there all along.

The counselor's response served as a highly effective strategy for reducing the client's resistance to change and increasing her willingness to accept assistance. But if the counselor had said it either *strategically* (in a conscious effort to manipulate or use "reverse psychology" on her) or *sarcastically* (to communicate incredulity that she could deny and rationalize such an obviously self-destructive situation), then the response would have been nothing like the one Joyce actually made.

Joyce's reaction was evoked when the counselor suddenly let go of his own agenda, perspective, and judgment about the situation. No longer feeling threatened, Joyce experienced him as trying to take in and then communicate as fully as he could his understanding of her experience. His shift from a *counselor-centered* to a *client-centered* stance freed her to engage in a more genuine and open way and thus to recognize the seriousness of her situation and her desire to change it.

The principles inherent in the motivational approach just illustrated apply equally to any issue about which the client is likely to have powerfully conflicting feelings, including abstinence from a substance that the client may view as friend and support. Once the client-centered relationship and clinical focus we've described has been established, the counselor can incorporate without igniting resistance the other tools (e.g., education, advice, feedback, support) that are central to successfully treating substance abuse and dual disorders. The coming chapters will describe in detail and with clinical examples how this can be accomplished in a variety of settings and contexts, while reducing the frequency with which counselors spin their wheels like poor Henry and Liza or otherwise back themselves into a corner which neither counselor nor client can escape.

Chapter 8

Pretreatment Motivational Counseling

Introduction

The problem of treatment compliance begins with the first point of contact clients have with a treatment system: the initial request for help. Typically this involves a phone call from individuals who are responding to someone's perception—sometimes their own, but just as often their spouse's, parent's, or boss's—that their substance use is out of control or causing significant life problems.

In this chapter, we will describe a motivational intervention we developed to increase the chances that persons who make contact will come in for their crucial first appointment with a counselor. The intervention is not only effective, but it is easy to use and it adds little extra time (no more than ten minutes) to the usual phone call. Its value lies in reducing the number of callers whose first contact also turns out to be their last: those individuals we have come to think of as "ghost clients."

The Problem of the Ghost Client

Every counselor who works with substance-abusing clients and has been involved in the intake process has had this experience: a person calls and says that he's in trouble with drugs or alcohol and needs help. With interest and concern the counselor draws the caller out, and soon the counselor is hearing the whole sordid story: the caller's misery, his lies and irresponsible behavior and the people he's hurt, his whole world falling apart and not knowing where to turn, the loathing and disgust he feels for himself when he thinks of what he's done, the thoughts of just wanting to go to sleep and never wake up. . . . The counselor listens with compassion and a firm sense of what's needed; the caller is told that help is available, that at the treatment center they know what he's going through, that he should come in at such and such a time for evaluation and assistance, and that, in the meantime, he should find an AA or NA meeting to start dealing with the problem one day at a time. The caller agrees to do this and hangs up . . . and never arrives for evaluation.

Or consider another version of this scenario: a person calls and says that, while she doesn't really think she has a problem with alcohol or other drugs, her husband (or boss or mother) has been telling her that she drinks too much, and to get him off her back she figured she'd go and talk to someone one time. The counselor begins to question the caller about her alcohol use: how much, how often, when; who else thinks it's a problem; whether she ever needs an eye-opener, feels guilty about drinking, or tries to cut back. Then the counselor tells the caller that her husband is right: the caller has a drinking problem (or she's an alcoholic); there is no cure, but abstinence is the one known treatment; the caller should come in to find out more about her problem (or disease). Startled, the caller agrees to come in, all the while protesting that she really doesn't think she has that kind of serious problem and that once they meet the counselor will understand this. The counselor warns the caller of the role of denial in addiction, referring to it as the "fatal aspect" that could lead the caller into jails, institutions, or death, and emphasizes the importance of the caller making it in for the appointment. They hang up. The appointment time comes and goes with no contact from the caller.

We think of these callers as "ghost clients" because they appear out of nowhere, inform us of their presence with sorrowful or frightening communications, and then are never seen or heard from again. They haunt us as counselors because we know that they're suffering and in trouble, yet we could not reach them. We are left only with lingering questions about what else we might have done.

A Motivational Approach

We found one way of answering these lingering questions in an adaptation of the work of William Miller and associates in the area of "brief intervention." In examining the different kinds of counseling approaches used for the treatment of alcohol problems, they discovered two interesting facts. When they compared the empirical evidence for their effectiveness at helping people change their drinking, no approach consistently beat what they grouped together as "brief interventions." These interventions varied in terms of how brief they really were (e.g., one session, a couple of sessions, or even a few minutes of advice from a family doctor), but in many cases they were as effective or even more effective than much more lengthy and involved interventions.[1]

They also discovered that, even though these brief interventions were done by counselors, therapists, and doctors with a range of orientations and theoretical approaches, all could be characterized in terms of six key components. And when they looked more closely at the brief interventions, they found that the more components each intervention contained, the more effective it tended to be.[2]

Miller and his colleagues concluded that the combined effect of the six key components was to increase the willingness of those who received the interventions to accept the seriousness of their problems and to recognize the need for change. Motivational Interviewing incorporates these components into a structure designed to maximize the counselor's impact on clients' problem acceptance by helping the client to remain nondefensive while discussing painfully difficult issues. Building on the success of their approach, we created a pared-down version of this structure to heighten callers' openness to the need for change and to communicate that our clinic would be a safe, respectful place to seek help in deciding how to accomplish it. (See "The Brief Telephone Intervention" on pages 140–145.)

FRAMES: Components of Effective Brief Interventions

Miller summarized his findings about brief interventions with the acronym FRAMES.[3] This stands for giving personalized Feedback to the client; emphasizing the client's personal Responsibility for change; offering direct Advice to change; providing a Menu of options for how that change might be accomplished; responding to the client with Empathy; and supporting the client's sense of Self-Efficacy. Examination of these components will clarify what makes each important for increasing a client's motivation to come in for an initial appointment.

Feedback

Feedback refers to some form of personalized information about the client's behavior or its effects on his or her life. It is presented in an objective, nonpressuring manner, so that clients are left to grapple with it and figure out what it means for them. This may involve (in more elaborate interventions) formal presentation of results of specific tests or assessment tools[4] or more informal "feeding back" of information, statements of concern or mixed feelings, or other self-motivational statements[5] the client may have made during the course of a telephone call. Either way, it is unlike feedback used to persuade the client to see things the counselor's way. This input is given with the assumption that what clients need is not to be persuaded, but to be informed, so they can make their own decisions about what is best and what they really want.

> CO: The questions I asked you about your drug use and some of the areas of your life where you might be having trouble suggest that you've had more severe health problems than 90 percent of the people who use cocaine. Does that sound about right to you?
>
> CO: So let me see if I've understood. You're pretty sure that you got more and more depressed the longer you smoked crack, and that it got you deep into debt and made you neglect your kids. You're not sure that you couldn't stop if you tried to, but you did continue to get high even when you knew that child welfare was watching you. Is that it?

This motivational approach differs considerably from the more traditional, confrontative style of feedback.

> CO: Your answers to my questions indicate that you're smoking more cocaine than 95 percent of all users. Do you know what that's doing to your lungs and your heart? You're lucky you're not dead yet!
>
> CO: You've been smoking crack every day, you can't pay your bills, and you're about to lose your kids. Don't you think this proves you're an addict and that you have to stop right now?

The motivational approach avoids using scare tactics, argumentation, labeling, and direct persuasion in presenting clients with information about themselves. It tries as much as possible to be specific, concrete, and personal. But what is the usefulness of this style of presentation?

For one thing, the noncoercive and nonjudgmental approach avoids the kinds of problems with resistance encountered in chapter 7. It keeps counselors from getting into unproductive arguments or soon-to-be-ignored advice giving with clients who are especially sensitive to pressure or control. It's one thing to use pressure tactics when the client is confined in an inpatient treatment facility (though even there it can be quite counterproductive). It's another thing to engage in such a conversation with a prospective client who can easily escape by hanging up the phone and never calling back. Using traditional feedback in this context lessens the chances of ever hearing from that client again.

But beyond avoiding such "roadblocks," giving concrete and objective feedback to a client who's just called can serve several other positive purposes. In order to present this information, the counselor has to have been listening closely. This often makes clients feel good, as does the realization that the counselor is taking their statements seriously. It also shows the client directly that the reason for asking all those questions and gathering some very private information was not merely to classify, analyze, or pigeonhole the client but to help the counselor get to know and understand the client better. This can be a remarkably powerful experience—like showing clients a portrait of themselves after having looked closely and made the effort to get it right.

Objective feedback, then, can lay the groundwork for treatment acceptance. But it can also serve the complementary role of establishing a greater level of problem acceptance. It heightens clients' recognition of the problem and the seriousness of their situation by re-presenting what clients have told the counselor in terms such as "dependence" or "abuse" or by providing information that they do not have. But even telling persons what they have just said can have a significant impact on how they see themselves. This may seem strange, yet everyone has had the experience of taking one's own words more seriously after hearing someone else repeat them back. Feedback begins to develop the discrepancy[6] between clients' goals or wishes and their current state, highlighting the distance between who they want to be and who they actually are.

Responsibility

The second of the components, *personal responsibility*, emphasizes both the client's freedom to make his or her own decisions about change, and the counselor's recognition that only the client can take the steps necessary for change. This reverses the more traditional assumption that substance-abusing clients are so impaired that they can no longer make decisions and must be forced to do what is good for them. Instead, the counselor starts from the premise that clients always make their own decisions. The goal is to help them make these decisions more in their own interest than they have up to this point. This counselor also avoids telling clients what their responsibility is or that they should start "being more responsible."

CO: I'm not going to be trying to make you change what you're doing, and, the truth is, I don't think I could even if I wanted to.

CO: I see that this is really a difficult decision you're facing, and I'm wondering if you've had any thoughts about what you wanted to do about it?

Compare this with more traditional messages about the client's freedom to choose.

CO: You're going to have to accept that your life is out of control and that your addictive thinking is what got you here. It's time for you to stop thinking and start listening to what others who've been there know will work. What you need to do is . . .

CO: You need to make some decisions right now about what you're going to do. You're the one who has to take care of this situation and accept responsibility for yourself.

By refraining from attempts to pressure the client to do what the counselor thinks best, the counselor avoids generating the twin forms of resistance discussed earlier—overt defiance or empty compliance—which might drive the client away. By resisting the temptation to moralize about the client's responsibilities, the counselor prevents the client from feeling "preached at." This component simply accepts the obvious: short of putting a gun to the client's head, the counselor really cannot make any client act as the counselor wishes, and the counselor's ideas about what the client should do, however well-intentioned, mean nothing if the client doesn't share them.

But again, this approach not only avoids potential roadblocks; it also serves to convey respect for the client's autonomy. Such respect is universally valued, as the exercise in chapter 7 illustrated, and there is an important ethical component in acting this way as well. But even on a purely practical level, there is a considerable advantage to this stance.

Persons with addictions often seem to have a heightened sense of independence. Many substance-abusing persons, for example, will put their "freedom" above all other things, including what most would consider reasonable restrictions (e.g., that one can't go wherever one wants on a workday, or be married and sleep around, or come home whenever one feels like it). It is surely the case that growth and change will involve a new appreciation for the way in which accepting limitations on certain aspects of one's freedom "frees" people to pursue what really matters to them: love, work, opportunities for creativity and play. But this is precisely the point: this appreciation will come only at the end of a process of change, not at its beginning. Expecting clients to accept, much less embrace, limits on their freedom before they really understand the payoff is unrealistic and a recipe for decreased treatment compliance.

Advice

If substance-abusing clients are especially sensitive to protecting their autonomy, it is because they have come to perceive the world as dedicated to undermining it. If they are to come to value their counselor's guidance, it will only be to the extent that they feel free to accept or reject it, and do not sense that the counselor is trying to influence them against their will. This is especially important to our intervention, because the third of the six components is *advice*. Clear recommendations are made to clients about the need for change in order for them to achieve their goals, and advice is given as to how this can be accomplished. Unlike the more traditional approach which provides early and unsolicited advice, however, the emphasis on the client's own responsibility for change positions the motivational counselor to offer suggestions that are experienced as offers of help with an undertaking of the client's own choosing.

CO: You've been telling me that you are worried about the effects of your cocaine use on your finances and your relationships. I would recommend that you stop using it altogether, because it has been our experience that efforts at limiting use are very unlikely to be successful.

CO: If you stop drinking now, there's a very good chance that your liver would return to normal, so that's what I would advise you to do. If you're interested, we can talk about how you might accomplish that.

The contrast with the more traditional style of advice giving is clear.

CO: The idea that you could cut down on your cocaine use is just a fantasy. You need to admit that you're powerless over it and start staying clean one day at a time.

CO: You've got to stop drinking now. With your liver in the condition it's in, to do anything else would be suicidal.

It is important for clients to know that the counselor does have a clear idea about what would help them to achieve their goals but that the counselor would not try to force this idea on them. Offering expertise conveys to clients the counselor's confidence in his or her ability to help them. It also, of course, gives clients concrete assistance in taking steps toward change while validating their own perception that change is necessary. To provide the (perhaps desperate, possibly isolated) client with a sense of hope that things can get better is one of the most important functions the counselor can serve, even in a brief interaction.

Expertise, however, need not be communicated with the assumption that the client ought simply to accept what the counselor says. Rather, to speak authoritatively requires a clear explanation of the reason for suggesting a particular course of action. If the advice makes sense to clients, their confidence in the counselor's judgment is increased and they are more likely to follow the directive.

Menu

The value of advice can be compromised if it is presented as the only way in which clients can accomplish their goals.

This stance tends to evoke both disbelief and defiance. Instead, successful brief interventions offer a *menu* of alternative approaches and encourage clients to choose one that fits their particular needs and strengths.

CO: There are many ways that people have been successful at stopping their illicit use of painkillers. If you'd like, I can tell you about some of the options that are available and we could discuss which one might work best for you.

CO: You've been telling me that one of the hardest things about the idea of not drinking anymore is how worried you are that you'll end up alone most of the time. While there are lots of ways for people to quit, it sounds as though it might be really helpful for you to become involved in a self-help support program. Let me tell you about some of the different kinds of groups there are around here, and you tell me what you think about them.

This sounds quite different from the standard approach.

CO: With your level of use, you really need to be in rehab. Let me see how quickly we can get you in.

CO: Addiction is an incurable disease, but there is one known method of recovery: attendance at a Twelve Step program and working the steps with a sponsor. You need to start with ninety meetings in ninety days.

One of the most exciting developments in the addictions field in the last fifteen years has been the explosion of new treatments with demonstrated effectiveness. People with alcohol problems have been shown to benefit from assertiveness training, behavior contracting, motivational therapies, behavior modification (Community Reinforcement Approach), and cognitive-behavioral approaches (e.g., Relapse Prevention), to name a few;[7] new pharmacological agents such as naltrexone (ReVia) and acamprosate have shown great promise. People with heroin addiction have been helped by both cognitive and psychodynamic therapies,[8] as well as by modified motivational interventions;[9] innovative treatments for cocaine and other addictions continue to be developed and refined;[10] special treatments for dual-disordered clients[11] and other specific populations have been developed as well. And from the successes of Alcoholics Anonymous have grown a whole range of self-help programs (e.g., Narcotics Anonymous, Rational Recovery,[12] Moderation Management[13]) to fit a range of preferences and beliefs.

Offering options, rather than insisting on a single "right way" to achieve sobriety, allows clients to choose treatment rather than having it imposed on them. In fact, the evidence suggests that the experience of choice increases commitment. This approach also gives the client the experience of being treated as an individual with specific needs, rather than of being lumped generically in some category of "addicts" or "alcoholics." And because people achieve change in myriad ways, our stance has the added benefit of being true.

Empathy

The focus thus far has been on the content, or the "what" of the intervention. A specific kind of process, or the "how," which has been implied, can now be made explicit. The heart of the effective brief intervention is the relational style known as *empathy*: accurate understanding of the client's subjective experience is reflected back in a warm, nonjudgmental manner.

CO: When you look at the things that you've been doing, the ways you've been treating people you care about, the situation you're in, it's pretty overwhelming. In fact, you feel so bad about yourself that you start to think that maybe it's just not worth it to try and face it all.

CO: It's really frightening to think about the risks you've been taking lately, just to get high.

A more traditional counselor might respond differently.

CO: Only an addict could be in such denial about the damage he's doing by going on using. Maybe you still haven't hit bottom yet.

CO: The reality of what you've been doing is finally starting to hit you. Now it's time to do something about it.

Empathic responding does not refer to being sympathetic, nice, or agreeing with the client. Psychologist Carl Rogers, the founder of the client-centered approach to counseling, spoke of empathy as maintenance of the "internal frame of reference";[14] it is the ability to understand the client's experience "from the inside," as if it were the counselor's own, and to refrain from judging it as right or wrong or comparing it with some external or objective standard. Empathic responding involves communicating this deep understanding to the client, accurately and without adding the counselor's own viewpoint, usually through the technique of mirroring back the client's words, thoughts, and feelings known as reflection.

At a minimum, empathic listening conveys a consistent interest in and respect for the client's perspective, which is likely to contrast positively with responses the client typically receives from others. By the time they have sought treatment, most substance-abusing clients have generated tremendous anger, disappointment, and sorrow in the people around them. The reactions they are getting probably include berating, nagging, lecturing, criticizing, and threatening, which from the perspective of the significant others may well seem deserved. The counselor's relative detachment from the effects of the client's behavior allows him or her the special luxury of empathizing without needing to respond personally or actively to the behavior. The very rarity of such responses in the client's life sets the counselor apart in a positive way, as a person the client is likely to want to spend time with.

Beyond this favorable contrast, a consistently empathic style helps to create for the client what the analyst Roy Schafer has called the "atmosphere of safety."[15] We emphasized earlier how clients' defensiveness often reflects their expectation of being mistreated in some way. We've also seen that they may evoke from others (including treatment providers) exactly the kind of treatment they most dread. Realizing that the counselor is not going to respond with hostility or neglect, clients begin to let down their guard and speak more genuinely about their real concerns and beliefs. This is especially true of the absence of any shaming statements on the part of the counselor. As well known as substance-abusing clients are for their sensitivity to shame, their bravado and apparent indifference often seem to elicit just those kinds of responses.

The paradoxical nature of personal change is evident in this contrast: when clients find that the counselor is willing to accept them as they are, they begin to think about changing; whereas, when clients perceive that the counselor expects change, and thus does not accept them as they are, they experience "conditions of worth"[16] that leave them feeling unsafe and guarded, and needing to maintain a facade intended to hide the "defects" that make them unacceptable. The ventilation of feelings, which brings relief; the experience of being cared for, which brings hope; the acceptance of limitations, which brings change—all bloom with the empathic counselor.

Self-Efficacy

In the context of such an encounter the client recognizes the existence of a problem and begins to consider the need for change. At this point there is one further obstacle to overcome: if clients believe they lack the ability to achieve their goals, they are likely to retreat instead of move forward. The final component, then, of the effective brief intervention is support for the client's *self-efficacy*.

CO: It sounds as though you've succeeded in the past when you felt you had a lot of support for your efforts. Now that your wife has really gotten behind you, I think you're in a pretty good position to do this.

CO: I bet it wasn't easy for you to talk to me this way. What gave you the courage to do it?

The message from the more traditional counselor is often a different one.

CO: You have to accept that you can't do this on your own. If your pride gets in the way of asking for help, you'll end up right back where you started.

CO: Everyone has a different "bottom." I think you're calling because you finally hit yours.

The concept of self-efficacy might be thought of as the cognitive component of optimism or hope. Psychologist Albert Bandura found that the greatest influence on people's belief in their ability to succeed was their history of successes and failures.[17] Many clients call, of course, trailing a long string of failures, some old and some recent; they may be on the verge of more (e.g., loss of job, marriage, health) as well. For these clients, the idea of setting out to accomplish what might be the hardest thing they've ever tried—and to do it without the substance, the source of support and assistance they've most treasured and relied on—is an intimidating prospect. Their instinct may well be to avoid what could be yet another humiliating failure, which in their minds would force them to appear (to themselves as well as to the counselor) as incompetent, weak, and pathetic. Thus, they might retreat from any pressure they feel from the counselor and refuse to face their problems—the stance known as "denial."

Helping clients build a sense of optimism about the possibility of life improvement increases the likelihood that they will risk venturing into the unknown (i.e., treatment, substance-free living) rather than recoil from it. Counselors can do this most effectively by recognizing and affirming their clients' real successes, both in treatment and outside it.

The Brief Telephone Intervention

The goal of the first phone contact with new clients is not to motivate them to change addictive behavior, but simply to motivate them to arrive for the first visit and, if possible, to increase their receptiveness to what treatment has to offer. In deciding to adapt the FRAMES schema to this purpose, we took what seemed the most straightforward approach: to create an intervention that incorporates all six components, we wrote a structured dialogue (i.e., a script) that followed them point by point.

This dialogue was designed originally to come at the end of a long questionnaire, which was already being used to prescreen clients for appropriateness for inclusion in a treatment research study. It would be equally effective, though, following a brief period of information gathering about the client's substance use and other current concerns, as illustrated below.

CO: Hello, Alcohol and Drug Treatment Center.

CL: Uh, yeah, I, uh, I think I need to talk to someone about some problems I've been having.

CO: Sure. Can I ask your first name?

CL: It's John.

CO: Hi, John, I'm Judy. Could you tell me a bit about the problems you've been having?

CL: Well, I've been drinking a lot lately, and I'm not sure if that's really a problem or not, but a lot of stuff has been going on and I feel like it's getting kinda crazy.

CO: So there are a number of areas of your life that aren't going well and you're worried about. You've been drinking more than you used to, and you're not sure what role that's playing in all of this, but you're concerned enough to have called us to see if we might be able to help in some way. Is that it?

CL: Yeah, that's about right.

CO: Well, John, I wonder if I could ask you some questions about some of those different areas to get a better idea of what's been going on. You mentioned that you've been drinking a lot lately. Could you tell me more about that?

At this point the interviewer can gather information about the caller's drinking and, if relevant, other substance use as well. This can be done informally, through the use of a formal screening device,[18] or according to the specific needs of the agency or institution. It is important for the interviewer to ask for any negative consequences of the alcohol or other drug use that the caller is aware of. This can vary widely according to the substance. A heavy drinker may not connect other life problems with drinking, but someone who has been smoking crack cocaine may reel off a litany of areas in which the drug has been destructive. It is also extremely important that the interviewer ask about other areas of concern in the caller's life. Even if it seems that all the problems are obviously related in some way to substance abuse, at this point the caller is unlikely to see it that way. To show interest only in the caller's use of substances is likely to alienate the caller or to leave him or her feeling misunderstood.

Once the interviewer has sufficient information to recommend that the caller come in for further assessment, the structured intervention begins.

Feedback

CO: John, I'd like to take a couple of minutes to sum up what we've been talking about. It sounds like alcohol has had some pretty serious effects on your life. You've said that . . .

Interviewer reviews problems and negative effects—health/physical, legal, social, familial, occupational/financial, emotional/psychological—specifically identified by the caller.

Also, I can tell you that, from a professional standpoint, you do fit the profile of someone whose use of alcohol has become reason for concern. You've noticed . . .

Interviewer reviews diagnostic criteria for dependence or abuse met by the caller (tolerance, withdrawal symptoms, unsuccessful efforts at cutting down or quitting, using more or longer than intended, a great deal of time spent obtaining/using/recovering from using, continued use despite negative consequences, other activities given up or responsibilities unmet).[19]

Is this how you see it, John? How does all this sound to you?

Interviewer reflects statements by the caller that acknowledge the existence of a problem, express concern about current behavior, or indicate thoughts about making a change. Interviewer highlights any recognition of differences between how things are and how the caller wants them to be; reflects both sides of the caller's ambivalence about what to do (e.g., wanting to make a change and at the same time wanting to go on drinking or using);[20] *remains nondefensive if the caller objects to anything the interviewer has said.*

Responsibility

CO: So it seems that you do see your alcohol use as a problem for you *[if the caller has openly expressed ambivalence, the interviewer adds, "Even though you still have some questions about it"].* That's the most important thing, because you're the only one who can make the decision to try to deal with this and to take steps to make things better for you. What are your thoughts right now?

If a wish for change and/or a need for help are expressed, or the caller is simply hesitant, the interviewer continues to the next component.

If the caller minimizes the situation's seriousness or actively resists continuing, the interviewer elicits objections; reflects responses, and highlights the ambivalence being expressed (e.g., wanting things to improve but feeling unsure about making lifestyle changes); restates reasons for concerns; then continues to the next component.

Advice

CO: I think you made a good decision in contacting us, John. Our experience tells us that people with problems like the ones you've been describing have a better chance of solving them with the help of a professional treatment program. I'd suggest that you come in for a fuller, personalized evaluation of your situation so that we can recommend specific options to help you. Can we set that up?

Interviewer schedules the appointment, gives directions, clarifies arrangements.

You know, John, we find that sometimes obstacles come up which get in the way of people coming in for the next step, even with the best of intentions. How can we help make it easier for you to do this?

If the caller presents specific obstacles or asks for specific assistance, the interviewer offers help if it's available or discusses options if the agency cannot assist directly.

If the caller is noncommittal or unresponsive, the interviewer suggests possible obstacles (e.g., transportation, child care, work-schedule conflict); asks if any apply; then offers help or discusses options.

Menu

CO: John, I want to be sure you understand what we're going to be doing when you come in.

Interviewer briefly explains the initial assessment process and exactly what is going to happen when the caller arrives for the appointment.

From what we've been talking about, I think that our program could be very helpful to you. But, we want to meet with you in person to be sure and to explain to you what we have to offer and how it all works. Once the evaluation is done, the counselor will tell you what your options are and what we recommend. Of course, it'll be up to you to decide if it's what you need. Does that make sense? Do you have any questions about anything, anything you're unsure of?

Interviewer answers the caller's questions.

Empathy

CO: I can imagine how difficult things are for you right now, John, and I bet it wasn't easy calling us up and talking about all this to a stranger.

Interviewer responds with reflection either to caller's confirmation or denial of this.

Self-Efficacy

CO: I think it's really important that you did take this step, though, and my experience tells me that you'll probably be able to take the next one, too, by coming in to see us, especially since we've dealt with some of the things that could have gotten in the way.

Interviewer responds with reflection to the caller's response, especially expressions of confidence about making it in for the appointment.

OK. We'll be looking forward to seeing you on _____ at ______ . Good-bye.

Chapter 9

Transitional Motivational Counseling

Inpatient to Outpatient: The Difficult Transition

You are in an institution of some kind. Your choice to be there was made, at best, as the least of all available evils; at worst, under duress and the threat of losing what matters to you most—your job, spouse, children, freedom, sanity, or hope. Once there, your awareness of the possibility of renewal through this trial of the spirit exists side by side with the cold, hard slap of the reality that your behavior is controlled and your movements limited by forces outside yourself. You are told, and deep down you know (whether or not you admit it out loud, or even to yourself), that you must make the most of your time in this place if you are to have anything like the life that you want. Yet to be here, locked up, is a humiliation, an experience of being reduced from the complex and unique person you imagined yourself to be to some lowest common denominator or category: "alcoholic," "addict," "mental patient."

Time passes and, despite the damage to your pride (or perhaps, in part, because of it), you begin to rise from the depths of sorrow, anguish, and mortification toward something lighter, cleaner, a small wisdom tinged with sadness and regret. Your mind begins to clear, your thoughts come more rapidly (or perhaps more slowly and without pressure); your mood begins to lift and you start to think that, just maybe, you are going to survive this ordeal with your selfhood intact. You begin to think of how great it's going to be just to leave this all behind, like a bad dream that leaves you with a vaguely uneasy feeling but (mercifully) no more than fragments of the events you've gone through or witnessed. And then, someone comes to you and tells you that it's really not all over: while you will no longer be physically restrained, you will be required (or strongly encouraged) to repeatedly visit, for some unspecified but apparently lengthy period of time, a version of the place you're about to leave. In fact, you are told that, if you do not comply with this recommendation, you are likely to find yourself back in this very same nightmare again at some later (but not too distant) date.

To say that you find yourself between a rock and a hard place is certainly to understate the case. Yet the whole thing is treated as though it's the most routine thing in the world—and the message comes across, loud and clear, that for you to act as though it's not is already a sign of dire consequences to come.

It is certainly true that for some who enter rehab, residential treatment, or acute care psychiatric facilities, the prospect of participating in "aftercare" is overall a positive one. These individuals see aftercare as an opportunity to build on the progress they've made during the weeks of inpatient care, and they may even value aftercare for its potential to provide a more individualized treatment than the one offered to large groups of residents. This chapter is not about these individuals, as counselors may need to do little to ensure that they will follow up with aftercare. Counselors simply can give them the appointment and open the door.

On the other hand, it is also indisputably true that, for another large group of individuals completing an inpatient stay, the progression from denial to the beginning of acceptance is far too optimistic. These individuals may have gone to the groups, completed the assignments, and otherwise given the appearance of participation. Yet, as the end of their stay approaches, they may remain resistant to the idea that they have the kind of problem that requires such intensive intervention, much less ongoing attention and assistance. Chapter 9 is about this more difficult group of candidates for aftercare. They are the ones for whom the prospect of continuing in treatment represents at best an extension of a painful (if productive) experience, and at worst a repetition of a season in hell.

In our outpatient substance abuse and dual disorders clinic, we found that as few as one out of three patients discharged without intervention from our affiliated hospital actually showed up for their first aftercare appointment. As one would imagine, the numbers dropped off from there, so that by the end of the first month we were seeing a very small percentage of all those clients referred from our own inpatient unit. And yet, as we have discussed in earlier chapters, the failure to follow through with aftercare is a solid predictor of a range of negative consequences for the person who's been discharged.

We realized, then, that we had to find some way of at least getting these clients in the door, so that we would have the chance to show them what role aftercare could play in their ongoing recoveries. At the same time we knew that, given the limited resources of a clinic serving a largely indigent population, our approach had to be brief and efficient enough to be implemented on a widespread basis without breaking the bank. And so we came up with the single-session intervention that we'll describe in this chapter.

We have performed this intervention now with well over a hundred clients over an extended period. We have done it in groups and one to one, on the hospital unit and in our own offices at the outpatient clinic. Though the amount of improvement in first-session compliance varied with setting and context, we found that overall we almost doubled the number of clients arriving from the hospital compared with those who got only the usual discharge planning session from the inpatient staff. This chapter reviews that intervention and illustrates the forms it may take in practice.[1]

The Transitional Motivational Counseling Session: Overview

The Transitional Motivational Counseling (TMC) session is a semistructured intervention that integrates the FRAMES structure with the models of Relapse Prevention and Dual Disorders Recovery Counseling.[2]

In essence, the counselor's goal is to create, through empathic understanding of clients' experience, a safe atmosphere in which to explore clients' thoughts and feelings about aftercare. Counselor and client discuss the factors that led to the inpatient stay in order to support clients' concerns about how their lives have been going and thus increase motivation for change. Drawing out and highlighting clients' own hopes for the future, the counselor supports their belief that they will be able to achieve their goals and shows how aftercare can potentially play an important part in this process. Throughout the session, any recognition of problems or the need for help is affirmed, as are expressions of optimism and intention to act on these recognitions. On the other hand, overt objections are responded to nondefensively, and resistance is taken in stride. At the same time as the counselor offers advice to participate in aftercare, as well as a rationale for this advice and information about what successful participation requires, the counselor also emphasizes the client's freedom to choose whether to go forward with it or not.

We conduct the TMC session a few days prior to the client's discharge from the inpatient program. At this time the client's thoughts are naturally turning to what comes next, and irritability, somnolence, cognitive confusion, and other symptoms of withdrawal that tend to interfere with sustained interaction will have diminished enough so that the client is able to participate fully. We suspect, though we base this more on clinical intuition than hard data, that the very short inpatient stays associated with the pressures of managed care may make the intervention more difficult for the counselor; nonetheless, our experience thus far has been that it remains worth doing even under these adverse circumstances. Though TMC can be done in small groups (two to four clients), we will describe the session as though it were being conducted one to one, which we have found to be its most effective setting.

Introduction: Setting the Agenda

The counselor begins the TMC session by asking for the client's understanding of why they are meeting, clarifying the counselor's wish to discuss the transition from inpatient treatment to the aftercare program the client's primary counselor is recommending, and asking whether it's OK for them to talk together for half an hour or so. (In a small group, this is usually extended to about forty-five minutes.) We have found that it is a mistake to assume that the client has been provided with a clear explanation of the purpose of the meeting by inpatient staff, who in the course of fulfilling their various duties may be more in the habit of telling clients what to do and where to go than telling them what an assignment is all about. It has also been our experience that clients may, for various reasons (e.g., feelings of overstimulation and being overwhelmed by the inpatient experience; cognitive impairment caused by substance use; high general levels of treatment resistance), fail to take in or simply forget much of what they have been told.

Whether either of these is true, or whether the client does in fact know why they're meeting, the counselor's asking about the purpose of the meeting communicates from the first moment of contact an important message: that it matters to the counselor that the client understands what is happening, that the counselor will not expect the client to just go along without his or her "informed consent," and that the counselor wants the client to be actively involved in a discussion rather than to passively receive information or instruction. Asking about the purpose of the meeting also allows the counselor to set the agenda for the session without leaving the client feeling coerced or imposed on, a key factor in defusing any resistance that may be present before they even sit down together.

The Current Treatment Episode: Establishing the Context

Once the agenda has been established, the counselor asks the client about the circumstances surrounding the client's coming into treatment. In many cases, clients will be more than willing to talk about the events that resulted in their being there. In fact, the counselor may have to limit the recital of details or the pouring forth of the story in all its twists and turns. The counselor's task at this point is to listen intently and to accurately reflect back to the client the essential aspects of the client's story, especially what the client sees as the most important factors contributing to the inpatient placement.

CO: What brought you to rehab, Jim?
CL: Um, crack, mostly.
CO: Uh-huh, and how did crack lead you here?
CL: You know the story. It just got out of control and I had to do something, so I came in.
CO: Well, it's certainly true that that's a common story—starting to smoke crack and then having it take over. But I wonder if you would tell me a bit about how it happened for you.
CL: I started about three years ago. At first it was just once in a while, with a couple of beers. I really wasn't worried about it. Then I got into it more, and I started selling on the side because I couldn't afford it otherwise. Pretty soon I was missing work, going on three-day runs on weekends and then crashing. My boss got mad and said he didn't want to lose me, but if I didn't do something I was gone. So I picked up the phone.
CO: So when you first started to use, it really didn't seem like a big deal, until you got into it more heavily and started doing things you wouldn't normally do.
CL: Yeah. Selling drugs, that's not me.
CO: And since you said your boss didn't want to lose you, I'm guessing that missing work really wasn't you, either.
CL: Right. I was always on time, never sick. I'm the best worker he's got.
CO: Sounds like you're really proud of that. But there you were, ready to lose it all.
CL: *(Nods)* That crack really kicks your butt.

It is critical that the counselor allow clients to express themselves fully in describing their situation, and that clients have the sense that the counselor is genuinely interested in their perspective. Often clients will, by this point, have had many encounters in which they were told how to understand their current predicament; while they may have come to accept this view at least in part, they will likely be relieved and gratified that someone seems to be interested in their own understanding. Such full expression will also provide the counselor with important information about the key elements in the client's descent into the unmanageable existence he or she had arrived at prior to treatment. This information can be used later in the session to underline the need for change and help in accomplishing it.

After gaining a clear understanding of the client's downward spiral, the counselor shifts the focus onto the client's experience during the current treatment episode. The counselor's goal is to affirm (through reflection) the client's positive experiences of treatment, the learning that has taken place, and the client's perceptions of the role these new understandings may play in his or her ongoing process of recovery.

CO: What's it been like here for you, Tanya?

CL: It's OK. They got a lot of people who know what they're talking about, I guess.

CO: Could you tell me about one of the ones who seemed that way?

CL: Well this one guy, Steve, he talked about the different ways people out there'll try to suck you back in again. There was one that sounded exactly like my sister, and I knew if she came to me that way I'd wanna go out with her, so I said that and we talked about how to handle it.

CO: Did you come up with anything that would work, do you think?

CL: Yeah, like how I could tell myself that she's the one

who got me started in the first place, which is true, and then think of being back out there trickin'.

CO: So one of the things that's been good about being here is really looking at what you're going to have to deal with when you get out, and getting some help in figuring out how to handle it.

At the same time, the counselor will also empathically reflect—rather than dispute, reinterpret, or explain away—any objections, frustrations, or outright rejections regarding the inpatient staff or program that the client gives vent to. Not only would confrontation or argumentation tend to create even greater resistance to the program and staff themselves, it would also place the counselor squarely on the side of the "enemy" whose encroachments must be defended against—exactly where the counselor doesn't want to be.

CL: A lot of these counselors, they just get off on telling people what to do.

CO: When you feel like somebody's bossing you around, you really resent it, and there have been times when you felt that way here.

Counselors with inpatient experience may have seen a warning signal while reading this last response. The term "splitting" describes the tendency of certain clients to play one important figure in their lives against another, as children may play one parent against another to get something they want. When done by adults in treatment, this often involves treating one authority figure as "all good" and another as "all bad." Splitting can create chaos and disagreement among treatment providers and enhance the client's sense of power and control as a result. Concern about the problems that splitting can cause is often so great that counselors are strongly cautioned to maintain a unified front against client "manipulations" and especially against any criticism of members of the treatment team.

This stance implies a negative view of clients who complain about their treatment and runs counter to the spirit of effective motivational counseling. While counselors cannot ignore the fact that some clients do seem to generate unusual levels of conflict wherever they go, we see this behavior more as reflecting a sense of helplessness and powerlessness than a malign intention to control or dominate persons or situations. The empathic stance, which, as we've stressed, tries to understand clients' behavior in the context of their own view of others and the environment, neither challenges nor justifies such behavior, and reflecting what the client says does not mean that the counselor agrees with it. Our goal as counselors is to communicate to the client that we understand the message that we've heard and that, given the client's own perspective and experience, his or her view of a particular event or situation makes internal sense, even if it turns out not to be the only (or the most constructive) way of looking at things.

Past Treatment Experiences: Making the Connection

The counselor's next step is to inquire about the client's previous treatment experiences. A review of any past residential or inpatient stays allows the counselor to subtly or directly underline the history and extent of the problems with which the client has been struggling, further raising the client's awareness of the impact of those problems.

CO: Jill, is this the first time you've been in the hospital?

CL: Nah. I was in a couple of times last year and the year before. I was also in rehab once and in one time just for detox.

CO: This is something you've been dealing with for some time now.

CL: Yeah, I guess it's been about four or five years that I've been drinking pretty heavy and getting depressed. I never expected it to come to this, though.

CO: Can you say more about that?

CL: Well, I always thought that I would stop drinking if it ever caused any real problems in my life. I told them the last time that they'll never see me again once I was out the door. But here I am again in this damn place instead of out there working and living my life.

CO: So when you think about how you've gone on drinking even though it means ending up in the last place in the world you'd ever want to be, it really makes you feel angry.

CL: Yeah, angry. And bad about myself, too.

The counselor then inquires specifically about past outpatient or aftercare episodes, asking the client about them in detail: where the client was referred, for how long, what the treatment involved, what benefits the treatment provided.

The ensuing dialogue can go in a number of possible directions, each useful for helping the client make the connection between aftercare and life improvement. In some cases, the client will speak glowingly of a former counselor or treatment program. In these instances, the counselor's job is simply to reflect this perception back to the client, to affirm and reinforce the connection that already exists.

CL: Well, I was involved for a while in that program downtown, with this guy Darnell. He was a really good guy, you know. He listened to me and gave me some good advice. I even started working again when I was seeing him.

CO: When you think about the time you spent in that

program, with Darnell, it really seems that your life started to get better as you were meeting with him.

Often, however, the client will tell of having dropped out of treatment after a while or right after starting, or even of never having made the first appointment. One benefit of discussing the client's disuse of aftercare in such cases is that it often allows the counselor to demonstrate, rather than merely to assert, the connection between absent or insufficient follow-up treatment and the worsening or recurrence of the problem for which the client sought help.

CL: They told me I should go to this outpatient program, but I lost the paper they gave me and I missed the appointment, so I just kind of forgot it.
CO: How did things go for you after that?
CL: I did OK for a while, but then I started spending time with my old friends, and pretty soon I was using again.
CO: You said you did OK for a while. What were things like then?
CL: Well, it was only a couple of weeks. I guess I wasn't thinking much about what we talked about in rehab once I got out.
CO: So at least that one time, when you left rehab and didn't do any follow-up, it didn't take long before things went back pretty much to the way they were before. What do you make of that?

The other important purpose of discussing a client's disuse of aftercare is to draw out and assess the factors that contributed either to the client's decision not to engage in treatment or the client's failure to benefit from it. As we've detailed in earlier chapters, there is a wide range of possible reasons for which clients become noncompliant with treatment. The counselor's goal at this point is to help the client recognize which of these played the greatest role in the decision to drop out, and then to offer alternative solutions to problem situations.

> CO: When you look back at it now, Susan, what do you think got in the way of your keeping up with your outpatient appointments?

One group of clients will agree that aftercare is important, yet will have shown in past episodes only limited commitment to treatment. This may, in turn, reflect doubt or uncertainty about how aftercare can really help them, a lack of understanding of outpatient treatment, a more general difficulty in sticking with things once they've been started, or some other unacknowledged reservation about the process. Whichever it may turn out to be, what matters is to identify the obstacle and, if possible, to seek ways of overcoming it.

> CO: Brian, you mentioned that you thought it made sense last time when your counselor suggested coming to see us after you left rehab, but you never did come to the appointment he made for you.
>
> CL: I was going to go there, but other things I was doing just got in the way, you know? It wasn't that high on the list.
>
> CO: Following up really didn't seem all that important to you then.
>
> CL: Well, it's not that I didn't think it was important. I just didn't see what difference it would make.
>
> CO: At that point you didn't see what aftercare could do for you, so it's not surprising that you didn't follow through with it. What do you think *would* have made a difference for you back then?

Another group of clients may have been reluctant to commit to aftercare in part because they weren't sure they wanted to maintain the changes they'd agreed on in treatment. This is especially true for clients who have ideas about continuing to use in moderation but have been pressured to accept an official goal of abstinence. The counselor's challenge with such clients is to convey the idea that aftercare can be used to sort out what they want to do and what will work for them as far as life improvement is concerned.

CL: I didn't see going for more treatment after I finished last time. I mean, I wanted to try it on my own for a while, see how it worked out.

CO: What made you think that would work better for you?

CL: Well, I get pretty tired of everyone telling me what to do, what kind of changes I have to make.

CO: And you were thinking that that would happen again if you went to your outpatient appointments. It sounds like, for aftercare to be helpful to you, you would have to have the final say in what you do and don't do.

CL: Yeah. I'm not saying I couldn't use some help, but it's my life, you know?

A third group of clients will have had outpatient experiences in the past where in some way their expectations were not met. One client may have thought that his treatment team would take care of all his problems and then felt betrayed when this didn't happen; another might have expected individual counseling but received only group therapy; another may have found counselors too directive, too laid back, or too busy to pay attention. With these clients, the counselor must try to discover the source of the client's disappointment, and then communicate the hope that the next aftercare experience can be more useful.

CO: You mentioned you went to another clinic for a while the last time you finished rehab. What was that like?

CL: Well, I saw this guy for about fifteen minutes about once a week, and he told me to go to meetings and not pick up the first one, then sent me to group where a bunch of people sat around and complained about their lives. Oh, and I saw some doctor for about five minutes for meds.

CO: It sounds pretty clear to me that this wasn't what you expected to find when you went to aftercare. What did you think it was going to be like?

CL: I don't know, maybe just someone who would listen to me for a while, tell me when I was making sense and when I wasn't, that kind of thing.

CO: So one thing that would be important would be to feel like your counselor would take the time to really understand what you're dealing with, and then give you some guidance in how to make sense of it all.

A fourth group of clients will present more practical obstacles as the reasons for their failure to continue with outpatient care. Although in some cases these are used as excuses to cover up the client's real, underlying objection, it is often true that a lack of transportation to the clinic, unreliable child care, limited finances, or conflicts with work or other schedules can be the main factor in keeping a client from following through. The goal in these cases is to identify the specific obstacle the client faced, and then to discuss viable solutions should it recur. If there were other, more significant reasons for the client's not following through, clearing away the practical roadblocks is likely to give the counselor greater access to them.

CO: Was there anything that got in the way of your coming in for your aftercare appointments?

CL: I didn't know how I'd get there.

CO: Uh-huh. What were some of the options?

CL: Usually I take the bus to get around, but some days I don't have the cash.

CO: What do you usually do when you have to get someplace important but can't come up with bus fare?

CL: Sometimes I borrow my brother's bus pass, but he

works the second shift and needs it back in the afternoon.

CO: So, if you'd been able to have morning appointments, you wouldn't have had any trouble making it in?

At the other end of the spectrum from these concrete problems is the broad issue of trust that often comes up, either directly or indirectly, in these sessions. For many clients, the prospect of opening up to a stranger about their most personal feelings and concerns is anathema. Revealing one's inner self may violate the "street" code of never showing vulnerability, go against family-of-origin rules about not airing dirty laundry in public, or recall a history of feeling rejected, betrayed, or mistreated by those in positions of authority. If clients do push themselves to put aside their mistrust temporarily and come in for aftercare, their sensitivity to slights, negative messages, efforts at control, or indifference on the part of the counselor may lead them to drop out without ever testing the accuracy of their mistrust, much less discussing it openly.

Clients often express this general sense of mistrust by asserting that they're "not the kind of person who asks for help." Male clients, especially, may insist that they've always taken care of themselves, never needed anything from anyone, and the like. While this is intended to communicate independence, it is easy to recognize the underlying belief that to "need" or to "take" from someone else is really a sign of weakness. These clients have maintained the illusion of self-sufficiency by turning to substances for gratification and emotional support. They believe that if they were to acknowledge the obvious—that no one is self-sufficient—then they would find themselves vulnerable to exploitation, injury, or abandonment.

While such difficulties cannot, of course, be resolved in this session, the counselor can express acceptance of a client's reluctance to share intimate secrets and suggest that coming to trust anyone, including a counselor, is a process that occurs over time rather than all at once. By communicating that this process is an individual one and cannot be rushed, and by avoiding the message that reluctance to open up is a character flaw or a form of interpersonal failure, the counselor gives the client permission to be mistrustful and yet still show up for appointments. In this way the powerful obstacle of mistrust may in time be overcome.

CL: I really didn't see the point of going for counseling. I wasn't going to tell someone I don't know my business, I mean the really personal stuff, but if you don't, then it's all just a joke.

CO: You're thinking that the counselor would have expected you to come right in and spill your guts, and there's just no way you were going to do that.

CL: No way. I'm a private person, and that's not going to change.

CO: If coming to counseling would mean that you had to give up your privacy, you'd really have no use for it. And you were not about to talk about anything that you're not comfortable with. My experience has been that many people feel this way when they first come to a counselor, and I certainly can't imagine any benefit from a person saying more than he wants to. I think that counseling is just like any other relationship this way. Of course, you wouldn't tell someone you just met your deepest secrets. But when you find the right person, after a while you want to talk about more than just the weather.

CL: Yeah, but how do I know I'd get the right person?

CO: Maybe that's part of what you were wondering the last time too? Whether the counselor you got would be the kind of person you might want to talk to? I wonder what kind of person the "right person" for you is.

Our final category of client reasons for not following through with aftercare focuses not on underlying feelings or concerns, but on *events* occurring in the course of treatment that precipitate sudden dropout. By far the most common of these in our experience is the missed appointment: the client fails to arrive for a scheduled session, does not make further contact, and disappears.

Most counselors would not see a single "no show" as reason enough for a client to stop coming altogether. Though annoying, client failures to attend scheduled sessions tend to be treated as part of the "normal" fluctuations in treatment compliance shown by substance-abusing and dual-disordered persons, and are best seen as further material for counseling work. (And, if the truth be told, many excessively busy counselors have breathed a sigh of relief to have an extra forty-five minutes from time to time to catch up on paperwork or phone calls.)

For many substance-abusing and dual-disordered clients, however, making contact after just not showing up for an appointment is something to be avoided, if at all possible. Some assume that the counselor will be so angry about this breach as to make further work together pointless. Others expect to be berated for what is certainly the umpteenth time about their irresponsibility or lack of consideration. Feelings of embarrassment (or even full-blown shame) over being exposed as a screwup or guilt for having let the counselor down or failed in (yet another) commitment typically accompany such expectations. In some cases, this triggers even stronger feelings: hopelessness about ever making real progress or defensive rage against life and the circumstances that conspired to prevent attendance. Regardless of the perceived problem, the client's solution is the same and consistent with the overall pattern of addiction: avoid the source of the bad feelings through withdrawing, and thus escape them.

There are, of course, clients who drop out without seeming to experience any of these feelings or even to give more than a moment's thought to their "decision." Though an extended discussion of this question goes beyond our purposes here, we would suggest that the apparent absence of expected reactions often masks and serves to deaden the pain of truly intense and excessive feelings of guilt and shame which, if experienced directly, would be more than the individual could bear.[3] It is precisely the ability of addictive substances to subdue these overwhelming feelings, we might add, that may make them so appealing in the first place.

These reactions are especially powerful when the reason for the missed appointment is not circumstantial, but has to do—as it very often does—with the client's having returned to using. In such cases, clients may well feel that there is no point to returning, either because they believe that the counselor will regard them with disgust or despair or because they themselves view the relapse as a failure or a sign of the impossibility of maintaining change.

It is especially important that such past experiences be identified and discussed during the TMC session, if they have, in fact, occurred. A pattern of giving up at the first stumble or moment of weakness or anxiety is a major risk factor for treatment noncompliance and may sap whatever hopeful or optimistic feelings the client has about things going better in the future.

CO: Todd, you mentioned that you were going to counseling for some time and then you dropped out. It sounds like that happened pretty suddenly.

CL: Yeah. I actually liked going for a while, but then I didn't feel like it anymore.

CO: What changed?

CL: Well, nothing changed, really. The program was still pretty much the same.

CO: I wonder what made you decide to stop going, then.
CL: I didn't exactly decide. I just didn't go back.
CO: Did something happen?
CL: Not really. I missed one of my sessions, and then I didn't go anymore.
CO: So your not going back had something to do with missing a session.
CL: Kind of. The thing is, I relapsed, and afterwards I figured I might as well forget it.
CO: Did you feel like the counseling wasn't helping, since you relapsed?
CL: No. I just figured he'd be pissed at me and I didn't want to deal with it.
CO: You expected your counselor to get on you about missing the appointment, or relapsing, or both?
CL: Both, I guess. I pretty much felt like a jerk anyway.
CO: So you felt pretty bad about missing that way, and for that reason, and you didn't need someone else piling on.
CL: I don't know. Maybe he wouldn't have beat up on me. I guess I didn't want to find out.

Looking Toward the Future: Considering Aftercare

Having discussed the client's current situation and past experiences, the counselor now shifts the focus of the interview toward its destination: the confirmation of plans for the future. By this point in the interview, the counselor has established at least a temporary bond with the client, and this is reinforced through inquiry about the client's hopes, plans, and expectations for life after discharge.

The counselor has two main purposes in this discussion: to help clients see how aftercare can help them to achieve their own goals, and to anticipate roadblocks likely to arise in the effort to follow through with aftercare and change.

The way has already been prepared for the second of these. Since the best predictor of the future is the past, it is likely that the same kinds of obstacles that led to premature termination of treatment in prior episodes will again threaten the client's progress. What remains is to see whether the client can identify constructive alternatives to the treatment-undermining behavior engaged in previously.

CO: You said that you'd really like things to be different this time, and that you think aftercare could be an important part of that. What might interfere with sticking with it, Donita?

CL: I don't know. I'll probably keep coming.

CO: I'm thinking about when you were telling me earlier that the last time around you started attending, and then you stopped going when you felt like your counselor said something you didn't like. Do you think something like that could happen again?

CL: Maybe. It depends on the counselor.

CO: Well, it's true that you don't have much control over what the counselor says, and it would be great if she's always right on the money. But what if she does say something that bothers you. Is there anything you could do to deal with that other than dropping out?

CL: Maybe I could tell her about it.

CO: How hard would that be to do, do you think?

CL: Pretty hard. I don't like to get into confrontations with people. Usually I'd just rather leave it alone.

CO: So even though it sounds like a good idea right now, it doesn't seem like just telling her about it would be so simple. What thoughts do you have about how to make it easier?

The counselor's other concern is to elicit from clients what they want once they're back to their regular lives. As we've discussed in an earlier chapter, counselors may confuse their own goals for the client with the client's goals, and only the latter will serve as genuine motivators for treatment compliance and change. While early recovery is the time to develop client goals in detail, it's still important in the TMC session to ask clients about what they would like their lives to be like, and especially how they'd like life to be different from the way it's been recently (or so far). This, in turn, will help counselors understand what kind of help clients believe they need.

CO: As you know, James, we're meeting because you're going to be leaving here soon and going back to your own life. I'm wondering what you think it's going to be like when you get home.

CL: I don't know. It's been a long time since I didn't wake up there and start the day with a beer.

CO: When you think about going home, one of the thoughts is about how strange and unfamiliar it's going to feel at first.

CL: But that don't really matter, because I'm just gonna have to get used to it.

CO: So you're really committed to dealing with the strangeness in order to stay sober. What makes that so important?

CL: Man, I'm sick and tired of messing up all the time, you know, not going to work, getting fired, being broke. I can't live like that no more.

CO: The way you're seeing it now, there's no way that you can keep your job and take care of your responsibilities if you're also drinking. And doing those things means a lot to you.

CL: I never thought I'd end up like one of those guys who didn't have nothing. I always wanted to take care of myself, like my Dad never did.

CO: You almost forgot for a while how much that mattered to you, when you were drinking.

CL: Yeah. But now I remember.

CO: Yeah. And I wonder where you see aftercare fitting in with that?

Bridging the Gap: Providing Information and Offering Contrasts

It follows naturally from the talk of client goals and the role of aftercare in achieving them to discuss just what is involved in aftercare treatment. One of the most common roadblocks to following up is adjusting to the aftercare setting. After finally getting used to the inpatient or residential program, the client is asked to start all over, with new counselors, new rules, and new surroundings. While this unfamiliarity cannot be eliminated, the counselor can help alleviate the client's nervousness by providing detailed, step-by-step information about how aftercare works (e.g., where the program is located, the hours of operation, how the intake process works, what treatment options and providers are available) and answering any questions the client might have. If the program allows for choices in terms of frequency of attendance, types of treatment available, or other aspects, the counselor should emphasize these choices and seek to match the program to the client's individual needs and concerns, as identified earlier in the session.

When this information has been provided and questions answered, the counselor shifts into the final phase of the TMC session: bridging the gap between inpatient and outpatient care by contrasting the two. The differences fall into two categories: the goals of treatment, and the method by which these are achieved.

The counselor tells the client that the purpose of inpatient or residential treatment is to take a person who is in crisis, whose life has spun out of control, and reestablish stability while preparing the person to resume life outside. Whether it's a three-to-five day detox, an acute psychiatric hospitalization, or even a two-to-four week rehab stay, only a limited amount can be accomplished in such a short period (relative to the long period of time the client has been using). The optimal outcome is that the client leaves with a new outlook, a new way of understanding life and its difficulties, and some familiarity with a set of tools that can be used to cope more effectively with life's challenges. The more common outcome (especially in this day of shortened inpatient and residential stays) is that the client is sober and no longer in acute withdrawal, and has a moderately clearer mind with which to use a variably understood or remembered set of attitudes and coping strategies.

This is all that can reasonably be expected from an inpatient stay—a jump start into dealing with "life on life's terms." (If more is accomplished, it's a bonus.) The purpose of aftercare, on the other hand, is to translate these initial gains into lasting change. Aftercare follows clients while they try to apply what has been learned in a safe, closed environment to the complicated, unpredictable world outside. It is unlikely that all will translate smoothly, just as it is unlikely that a new driver will go from the simulator to the road without a hitch. By coming to the aftercare program, clients get an opportunity to practice "driving" in lifelike conditions with an expert guide, and then to evaluate what works, what doesn't, and how to adapt accordingly. They may also get the chance to deepen their skills so that they can not only survive, but also thrive "on the road" and have a good time in the process.

Just as the goals of treatment vary from inpatient to outpatient care, so, too, do the methods and expectations. In rehab or the hospital, clients are watched over constantly. Their day is structured for them, and, if they're not where they're supposed to be, someone will assuredly redirect them accordingly. This is presumably what is needed when individuals have reached a point where they are no longer in control of their behavior—someone or something to step in and reestablish control for them. What is expected of clients, then, is that they will be compliant or *surrender* to the process, in the interest of getting back on their own feet. The advantage is that clients need not try to make decisions they are not prepared to make, nor face the demands of life unprotected. The disadvantage, of course, is that their lives and actions are for the moment not under their own control.

In outpatient or aftercare treatment all of the above is reversed. If there is to be structure in clients' lives, they must be the ones to build it in and follow it through. No one will come calling if they miss a meeting or are late for an appointment. This means, of course, that clients have tremendous *freedom*; whatever they don't like or prefer not to do they can simply disregard. (Even so-called coerced outpatient clients, who are under external pressure to attend sessions and maintain sobriety, are ultimately free to do as they wish as long as they are willing to pay the consequences.) The client is "in the driver's seat." But this also means that all of the *responsibility* for the client's actions lies in his or her own hands. Clients have the opportunity to harm themselves as well as help themselves, to undermine their recovery as well as strengthen it. What is expected—what is required if the treatment is to succeed—is that the client be *actively committed* to the process.

Closing: Offering Hope and an Invitation

Bringing the TMC session to an end, the counselor attempts to leave the client by "closing on good terms."[4] For our purposes, this means that, having discussed both the difficulties and potential benefits of aftercare in the context of the client's own wishes, the counselor can now affirm that the program offers the client a realistic hope of achieving those goals. The counselor may again invite the client to ask further questions. The counselor should communicate to the client, as long as this can be done sincerely, an affirmation of the client's participation in the discussion they've had together.

> CO: We've really covered a lot of ground together, Tina, and I want you to know that I appreciate how open you've been with me about your experiences. Is there anything more that you might be wondering about before we stop for today?

When the questions have been answered, it's time for the final step: welcoming the client to come to aftercare. If the session has gone reasonably well, this may seem like a formality, or even a redundancy, but it can be surprising how much impact a definite invitation at the end can have on the client's memory of the session and its outcome. If this somehow seems out of place, or the client refuses, this is a sign that somewhere along the way the counselor has lost touch with the client's concerns or reservations. If time remains it might be worthwhile to try to address this further, or at least to inquire as to the source of the hesitation. In most cases, however, the client will welcome the invitation and respond in kind. Though this does not guarantee that the client will indeed arrive for the first aftercare session, the chances of his or her doing so will have been dramatically increased by the counselor's intervention.

Chapter 10

Motivational Counseling in Early Recovery

Introduction

The preceding chapters in this section describe specific interventions to improve treatment compliance. They also reflect an entire way of thinking about the counseling process with substance-abusing and dual-disordered clients. This perspective differs significantly from other approaches in blending directive and nondirective, evocative and educative elements. Incorporating each of these elements provides a way of neutralizing "reactance" or resistance potential.

According to a recent review of the literature on matching substance-abusing clients with types of counseling, "patients who have strong tendencies to resist external control through oppositional behaviors do best when treated with nondirective or paradoxical therapies. Conversely, patients who exhibit more cooperative and less resistant reactions to external demands are more likely to benefit from therapies led and directed by the therapist."[1]

From our perspective there are two implicit mistakes in this analysis. First is the assumption that resistance potential is a permanent, invariant trait of individuals—an assumption we've argued against in this book. Second is the assumption that treatments must unavoidably fall on one end of the spectrum of "directiveness" or the other. Most traditional treatments have done just that—for example, the highly structured and directive cognitive and behavioral treatments versus the unstructured dynamic therapies. But if clients may be more or less resistant at different times or in different circumstances, and if counselors wish to be prepared to work with the widest possible variety of clients, then an approach that allows counselors to match their interventions to their clients' interpersonal style at any point in the counseling process will enhance counselors' effectiveness.[2]

In this chapter we will describe how the Motivational Counseling approach can be applied to the initial counseling sessions. By recognizing the need for flexibility and appreciating the fluidity of clients' willingness to accept direction, counselors can maximize their chances of engaging and retaining clients in treatment while increasing their motivation for change.

Giving Up the Habit of Expertise

Motivational counseling for early recovery requires a significant shift in approach from either the confrontational tactics of traditional addictions treatment or a purely educational, skills-and-solution-focused style. When faced with a new client, many counselors bring to the session a template of issues and factors that they expect to address. These may include such topics as amount of clean time; current recovery environment (including family, friends, living arrangements, neighborhood) and presence or absence of recovery support; formulation of a recovery or relapse prevention plan, including use of self-help programs (meetings, sponsor, phone numbers, book work); recovery risk factors (complacency/overconfidence, denial/minimization of addiction, wishful thinking/hopes of limited use, refusal to reach out/excessive self-sufficiency/isolation, willfulness/lack of a Higher Power); and, for dual-disordered clients or those using adjunctive pharmacological therapies, medication compliance, side effects, and effectiveness.

The counselor's role, in this approach, is to elicit information about these areas and then to educate, advise, and encourage the client to deal with them in the way the counselor knows to be effective and healthy. The counselor, then, is the expert on recovery—either a benign or a demanding one. The client, as the recipient of the counselor's expertise, has the job of believing in the counselor's expertise, applying it to his or her life, and reporting back on how it's working.

In motivational counseling, by contrast, the counselor faced with a new client takes up the role of companion or partner[3] in a process of coming to accept a need for change and identifying and pursuing personally meaningful goals. The counselor's template, as we've seen, is more one of process than of content. The counselor seeks to develop the client's trust through exploring problems and concerns from the client's perspective; to draw out the client's own mixed feelings about these situations; to encourage the client to consider the harmful consequences as well as the advantages of each choice; to communicate empathic understanding of the difficulty of such choices, while keeping the client focused on the conflict at hand; and to support the client's belief in his or her ability to make the desired changes.

In doing all of the above, the motivational counselor has presumably helped the client move from precontemplation through contemplation of the problem,[4] to the point of feeling ready to try changing his or her behavior in significant ways. The most striking difference between this approach and the more familiar ones is the amount of time spent prior to any talk or suggestion of solutions to the problem. This is true not only for the big issues (e.g., "Do I want to stop using drugs or 'stay stopped' now that I'm out of the rehab/hospital?" or "Do I want to make changes in how I think, deal with my feelings, interact with others, and cope with life's challenges?") but also for the small ones, that is, not only for long-term treatment goals but also for the steps toward these goals.

So, if a client, Andy, is committed to abstinence, but talking about missing the old friends he used to get high with, the motivational counselor does not proceed to educate him about triggers or "people, places, and things," or advise him of the dangers of giving in to the wish to see them, or recommend meetings instead. Rather, the counselor explores this issue from Andy's perspective, elicits his view of the advantages and disadvantages of seeing his friends, empathizes with his ambivalence while keeping him focused on it, and gently guides him toward a decision that he believes is in his own best interest. And if Sarah talks about how hard it is to control her anger, the counselor does not offer anger management techniques or point out how failure to deal more effectively with anger is likely to lead to relapse. Rather, the counselor helps Sarah to look at how she experiences anger, the thoughts and actions associated with it, and their positive and negative consequences on her mood, substance use, self-esteem, and important life goals. (If Sarah's explosiveness did not provide her any benefits—self-protection, keeping others at a distance when feeling vulnerable, feelings of power—she would presumably have found other ways of behaving long ago.)

The most basic belief underlying our approach is that all people, including those who abuse substances, have reasons for behaving as they do. These reasons may not make sense from the counselor's perspective, and in fact they may not withstand close scrutiny by the client. (For example, Sarah's explosiveness may generate hostility in those around her, making her less safe rather than more.) Engaging clients in this process of examining their behavior, the purposes it has served, and its unintended consequences motivates clients to address the issue at hand and makes clients want to return to see the counselor for more of the same.

It may also allow the counselor to offer education and advice—*after* the counselor has explored the client's viewpoint, and *only* when the client gives signs of wanting the counselor's perspective or concrete help. Thus, motivational counseling does not negate the importance of the counselor's having appropriate knowledge of recovery strategies and techniques;[5] rather, it puts that knowledge in its appropriate place at the *end* of a process of problem and treatment acceptance, and requires the counselor to use it mindfully and selectively. Thus, the motivational counselor must also sense when the client is ready to consider making a change; invite possible solutions to the problem from the client; help sort out which are most feasible and likely to succeed; offer specific advice if the client requests or invites it; elicit commitment to a plan for action; and affirm the client's ability to carry the plan through and communicate optimism about the potential for success.

Giving up the habit of expertise poses a real and subtle challenge. It requires counselors not to assume that they know what is best for the client, how recovery really must work for the client, or what the answer is to any given situation or question—no matter how much experience and knowledge they bring to the session. In addition to early, overt advice giving or directiveness, counselors must also refrain from responses that implicitly assume they know what's best or how the problems ought to be conceptualized. Even seemingly innocuous terms like "trigger" or "your recovery" should not be assumed to apply for any given client at the start of treatment, and counselors should introduce such terms with circumspection, taking care to find out how this client understands them instead of taking their meanings for granted.

To make this shift necessarily will leave counselors feeling uncertain and insecure, having put aside at least temporarily the knowledge and expertise they usually rely on in their work. When beginning to try out this style, counselors should not expect to feel natural or at ease. Like any new skill, motivational counseling will at first seem foreign, "not me," and will leave counselors wondering how they suddenly became so inept. If counselors focus instead on *not* doing what is most familiar, and start from the stance of *not* knowing what the client needs to do but wanting to learn from the client, this will initiate the crucial shift from which everything else follows.

Getting Started

Although the structure and feel of the initial session will vary depending on whether it is being done as aftercare or standalone outpatient treatment, the format of the session is still defined by the two prongs of our motivational schema: problem acceptance and treatment acceptance.

When the context is aftercare, one desired focus is on where the client stands with regard to the central problem or problems that contributed to the hospital or residential stay: substance use and, for the dual-disordered client, depression, manic depression, anxiety, schizophrenia, or other disorder. It's important to address these issues in the context of clients' perceptions: how do they currently understand their substance use and (if applicable) psychiatric disorder? Where do they stand on each issue in terms of stage of change: seeing it as a problem, planning to take certain actions to resolve the problem, already acting to deal with the problem, recognizing which parts of the plan are ineffective and considering alternatives?

When the context is an initial outpatient session, the central problems may or may not be so clearly defined. If they are not, then the first desired focus is on clients' perceptions of what difficulties have brought them in to seek help. While substance use will typically be among these, the counselor cannot assume that the client sees this as the central problem. The counselor's goal is to determine how the client sees the problems.

The second desired focus is the same in both the outpatient and aftercare contexts: to develop a sense of how the client thinks and feels about coming for treatment. To answer this question will involve understanding the client's expectations of helping or authoritative relationships in general, past experiences in treatment, and his or her beliefs about ability to succeed in treatment. In short, the initial session will cover much the same ground as the transitional motivational counseling session described in chapter 9.

The Opening

Motivational counselors must set this agenda without giving the client the impression that the counselor is going to forcibly take charge of treatment. Beginning the initial session with a structuring counselor statement helps to establish the desired relationship.

CO: We have about forty-five minutes together today, Peter. I know you were in the hospital, and I understand that it had something to do with cocaine and depression, though at this point I'm not really sure in what way they've been problems for you or how you see their role in your life and current difficulties. I'm hoping that we'll be able to talk together to come to some clearer

> understanding and to help you deal with these problems and address any difficulties that come up along the way. This might be a little different from what you were used to in the hospital, and I'd be glad to talk with you more about how this all works. Right now I'm wondering, though, about what's been happening since you've been back home?

Clients may respond in a number of different ways: they may launch into a description of the events that have occurred since discharge, a series of complaints about their current situation, an account of recent cravings or symptoms, or a paean to the wonders of sobriety. As the client responds to the counselor's initial question, the counselor listens with the goal of understanding exactly what the client wants the counselor to know. While attempting to convey an understanding as accurately as possible, the counselor also draws out and clarifies whatever remains confusing or ambiguous.

If clients speak of their goals, wishes, hopes, plans, concerns, or fears, the counselor encourages them to say more about these topics, as they are central to the process of change. However, the counselor makes no assumptions initially about the client's perception of the problem, and especially does not assume that, because the client has just left inpatient or residential treatment, he or she is committed to change or agrees with the prescribed goals. It may be, as we discussed in previous chapters, that the client merely went along with the treatment staff. It is also possible that the client's feelings or wishes have changed since discharge, having returned to an environment more supportive of the status quo than of change. Instead, the counselor encourages the client to elaborate on any general, vague, or "correct-sounding" statements to see whether the client is clearly committed, ambivalent, or dubious.

CL: Well, I know I have to make some changes. There's no question about that.

It would be easy to take this kind of statement at face value and assume it indicates a strong intention to change and possibly a wish for help in doing so. However, as the first goal is to engage the client in exploring his or her feelings and concerns, the counselor should pursue the specific meaning of the statement.

CO: What makes you so certain of that?

Here are two possible responses to this question.

CL1: Well, my health is suffering, it's destroying my marriage, and I can't pay my bills. I can't stand to see my life fall apart anymore. I just don't see any other way out.

CL2: Well, that's what everybody tells me, you know? That I'd better stop getting high.

Obviously, these two responses reflect profound differences with regard to the client's problem acceptance (and implicitly the perceived need for help) and call for different interventions.

CO1: I see. You're really aware right now of how much your cocaine use has been costing you, financially and otherwise, and you've decided you need to make some changes. How far have you gotten? Have you taken any steps toward improving things?

Here, the counselor has recognized that the client may no longer be merely contemplating change but may instead be ready for the next step. The counselor affirms the client's self-motivational statements via reflection and then proceeds to further assess whether the client is preparing to change, already taking concrete steps toward change, or perhaps not quite as certain as he or she sounds, that is, struggling mightily between wanting to change and feeling drawn back to old behavior. This assessment would then allow the counselor to tailor the session appropriately to the client's needs—helping either to solidify the commitment to change and clearing away obstacles or helping to negotiate a clear plan of action.

CO2: Other people in your life want you to change. Maybe they've even been pressuring you. What are *your* thoughts about this?

Here, the counselor has recognized that the client's apparent statement of commitment to change was in fact a defensive attempt to head off what the client expected would be pressure from the counselor to change. This is an example of how overt compliance can mask covert defiance. The counselor thus "rolls with the resistance" and "avoids argumentation"[6] over who is "right" (the client or the "others"). By asking instead for the client's viewpoint, the counselor builds an alliance which may in time lead to discussing the client's cocaine use and goals, and the ways in which the first impacts the second.

Early Topics and What They May Reveal

The counselor is prepared to follow the client into discussion of the two desired foci—problem acceptance and treatment acceptance—if these arise spontaneously in the early part of the session. However, since the client may take the dialogue in any number of other directions, it may also profit the counselor to keep in mind a number of useful "early topics" to be explored. These are meant to serve as useful ways of getting at the central issues and eliciting the client's perspective on his or her current situation, attitudes toward treatment, and beliefs about his or her ability to succeed at change.

These early topics will be familiar from the TMC session and will serve many of the same purposes in the initial outpatient session. Several are relevant only for aftercare. Early topics include the following.

- *What led to the client's hospitalization/rehabilitation stay?* Any initial understanding of the client's perspective on his or her difficulties, as well as information specifically related to substance use and (if relevant) psychiatric disorders, will emerge as the client describes the events leading to residential treatment.
- *What was the client's experience of the hospital/rehab like?* This topic may provide an understanding of the client's recent state of mind, attitudes and feelings about treatment, and motivation for change.
- *What has it been like since the client left the hospital/rehab?* Current concerns or preoccupations, intentions regarding action toward change, or roadblocks may all be revealed as the client speaks of his or her experiences since discharge.
- *What have past experiences of outpatient treatment been like?* Relevant in both aftercare and outpatient contexts, responses to this question will reflect the client's ability to maintain motivation for change, history of treatment acceptance, sense of self-efficacy, and tendency to attribute his or her behavior to external (i.e., people/places/ things) versus internal (i.e., mood states, cravings) sources. Likely roadblocks to treatment compliance in the present will be revealed as well in the treatment difficulties in the past.
- *What was the client's first group session like?* For settings where clients attend group counseling sessions prior to individual ones, exploring the client's experience of these sessions can help the counselor to gauge the client's initial treatment alliance and any obstacles

> to compliance that may arise in early treatment. It may also bring out useful information about the client's interactional style and how this affects his or her ability to develop satisfying relationships, a crucial issue for most individuals with substance abuse problems.

Exploring Goals and Hopes for Treatment

We have made the point repeatedly that clients' primary internal source of motivation for change will be the contrast between life as it is now and their own hopes, wishes, and dreams of how it could be. These ultimate or *life* goals (e.g., a satisfying romantic relationship, respect in the community, financial security, material possessions, professional accomplishment, physical well-being) reflect clients' central wishes and are most clearly revealed when they are asked to imagine how they might like things to be years from now.

Because we are neither matchmakers, financial advisors, nor career counselors, however, and because clients are usually not ready in the earliest sessions to address problems in their interpersonal style, life goals do not initially serve directly to drive the treatment. The goals that become central in these sessions will thus be the client's *instrumental* goals (e.g., achieving and maintaining abstinence, experiencing relief from symptoms). The achievement of instrumental goals must precede the achievement of life goals. Yet it is always important to remember that these instrumental goals are only compelling to the extent that they help clients get what they ultimately want and that a failure to connect these two kinds of goals can easily undermine treatment success. Put simply: unless clients see some ultimate benefit to abstinence from substances—relationship improvement, financial or professional gain, improved health and well-being—they are unlikely to continue with the strenuous efforts and sacrifices needed to maintain sobriety.

The counselor's job, then, is to help the client recognize which instrumental goals will maximize the likelihood of achieving life goals. Only the client's own goals motivate action; part of the counselor's work, therefore, is to help clients become more aware of their goals or wishes with regard to the treatment. And because client goals only motivate action when clients believe they can achieve them, another part of the counselor's work is to help clients develop that belief.

Preliminary understanding of the client's goals often emerges from the discussion of the early topics. In some cases, goals may remain implicit in the first session rather than clearly articulated. Clients may resist clearly stating goals, if they believe they must now act to achieve the goal but feel unready to make such a commitment.

CL: I've been feeling really lousy lately, really down, uninterested in things. I know a lot of people think it has something to do with my drinking, but I really don't think that's it. I just want to feel better.

CO: So other people have suggested that there might be a connection between your drinking and how you've been feeling, but you think something else is at the root of it. What kinds of things have you thought might help you feel better?

CL: Nothing, really. I don't really know what I want to do about it yet. I think I just want to try to figure it out first.

In other cases, clients will begin to elaborate on what they hope to accomplish in treatment once the counselor formulates the issue more directly.

CO: You mentioned that it was when you started missing work that you realized you needed to do something about your drinking and contacted the rehab. What were you hoping to accomplish by going there?

The client may respond in any number of ways to such a question. In some cases, the client's goal is clear and well-formulated: he or she wants to stop drinking, permanently, and is seeking help in accomplishing this.

> CL: I just couldn't go on that way anymore. I knew I had to quit drinking, and I knew I couldn't do it on my own, so I went in to get a running start.

In these cases, the counselor can use clearly formulated goals to model an alternative to the impulsivity or short-term thinking many clients display by connecting those goals with possible actions.

> CO: You were saying earlier that one of the things you used alcohol for was to keep going even when you were exhausted. If you go ahead with the idea of getting a second job to make some extra money, how might that affect your efforts at staying clean?

Similarly, the counselor may choose to encourage the client to consider the consequences of not meeting the goals he or she has stated.

> CO: If you don't manage to cut back on your workload as you said you wanted to do, what might happen then?

Of course, the counselor may also be inclined to offer specific advice as to how to achieve the goal. We would say that, as a rule, the initial session is too early to be offering such advice, as to do so might discourage the client from exploring and affirming problem and treatment acceptance.

On the other hand, experienced counselors are well aware that many motivations other than behavior change can lead someone to seek residential treatment: getting a spouse or boss to "back off," buying time, avoiding legal penalties, etc. And even when clients' motivation for seeking help is internal rather than external, their ideas about the changes needed to accomplish their goals may differ considerably from the counselor's.

> CL: I figured that if I went someplace where I couldn't drink for a month and, you know, got the alcohol out of my system, I could go back home again and start fresh. You know, go back to drinking just now and then instead of all the time.

Client-generated goals may not be what counselors would want them to be or what they think best for the client. When clients formulate goals that the counselor believes to be unwise or unsustainable, counselors typically leap to advise them of their "mistake." The motivational counselor, however, waits for the client to directly ask for advice or at least clearly indicate a need for assistance. This, in turn, usually requires the kind of reasonably well-established alliance between counselor and client that may or may not yet exist in the initial session. In general, then, the counselor's task in such instances is to help clients explore the goal in concrete terms, identify possible obstacles, support their efforts to achieve it, and then review their success or failure with an eye toward revision as needed.

The goal setting in the above example, however, raises an issue that requires more extended discussion due to the controversy it generates: the question of nonabstinence goals. When clients indicate a wish to "cut down" or use in moderation, the motivational counselor's response is to explore their ideas about controlled use: hopes of minimizing the difficulty of the change being considered and the anxiety that accompanies it; needs (for excitement, socialization, or symptom relief) that they believe they require substances to meet; wishes to maintain an image of themselves as capable of self-control rather than as "powerless" over substances.

These concerns are then balanced against the counselor's rationale for recommending abstinence, if that is the advice: the difficulty most individuals dependent on a substance have in maintaining (as opposed to just achieving) reduced levels of use, and the greater safety of abstinence; the legal risks if the substance is an illicit one; if the client is dual disordered, the risks of mixing medications with self-administered drugs, and the likelihood that even moderate use of substances may complicate the process of relieving symptoms.

Ultimately, the counselor's recommendation rests on the belief that abstinence would give the client the best chance of achieving the life goals expressed in the session. Having laid out the pros and cons of a controlled-use goal and discussed the client's ambivalence about change, the counselor will in some cases find that the client accepts the goal of abstinence. In these cases, it is especially important to emphasize that counselor and client can work together to figure out how else to meet the real needs and address the genuine concerns the client has expressed.

Not all such negotiations will end this neatly, of course. Many clients come for treatment believing that controlled use is a reasonable option for them. Counselors working in the motivational style are likely to run across more of these clients primarily because their clients tend to be less afraid to say out loud what they are thinking to themselves. When the client maintains a commitment to such a goal but does not seem averse to continued consideration of options, the counselor emphasizes that the decision always remains in the client's hands and offers "warm-turkey" options[7]—ways to move in the direction of abstinence without an initial commitment to it as a final goal. Most of the proponents of limited-use goals[8] emphasize the desirability of a period of abstinence even if the ultimate goal is moderate use. Ninety days is preferable, but even commitments to briefer periods can begin the process of exploring the advantages versus the disadvantages of abstinence and the client's ultimate wishes.

Whether or not the client is open to these considerations, the counselor's final position is that, whatever the client decides, the counselor hopes that they can continue to talk about how things go as their meetings continue. The client's initial goal may not be his or her final goal,[9] and the client's experience, carefully reviewed and discussed with the counselor, will provide the motivation for revision. However skeptical the counselor may be, it is preferable in such cases to take a wait-and-see approach[10] as opposed to insisting on a position that clients will experience as rigid and uncomprehending of their situation.

Working with the Client-Counselor Relationship

In many cases, the relationship between motivational counselor and client develops into an effective alliance for change without ever becoming the focus of discussion. As clients feel increasingly safe and understood, they become increasingly open and honest about their troubles and concerns and use the counseling sessions to work out their problems. This is what we referred to in chapter 7 as the "unobjectionable positive transference," or basic trust. This level of trust is often missing initially but may develop in the early sessions. However, there are times when the client is so clearly defensive and mistrustful that no amount of empathic reflection of concerns or ambivalences can overcome this. In these instances, the client's feelings about the counselor or the treatment they're engaged in must be addressed directly.

Unlike the psychodynamically oriented psychotherapist, however, the motivational counselor does not use the counseling relationship as a primary tool for teaching clients about the purposes and consequences of their ways of interacting with others. Rather, the counselor's goal is to identify the obstacles to creating a productive partnership with clients and to find ways of removing or at least minimizing these obstacles.

Two clinical examples may be useful in demonstrating how this might work in practice.

- Thomas, a man in his late forties, had been drinking to excess for twenty-five years and attending Alcoholics Anonymous meetings for fifteen. He had on several occasions been sober for as many as three years, but each time had relapsed and destroyed all he'd accomplished during his sobriety. When he began motivational counseling after a brief hospitalization for depression and alcohol dependence, he repeatedly expressed sharp skepticism about the usefulness of any program other than AA in helping alcoholics. He also criticized the appropriateness of antidepressant medication.

  Thomas' counselor spent much of their first session, and significant parts of the next two as well, addressing these concerns: empathically reflecting Thomas' reservations about psychiatric treatment, acknowledging his uncertainty about continuing and his right to make this decision for himself, and exploring what it meant to Thomas for the two of them to be meeting. This led to fruitful discussion of Thomas' beliefs about mental illness and his own suspicion that his relapses might in part have been related to his becoming depressed. When he revealed his fear that to accept this would call into question his faith in AA as "the solution" and thus leave him with nothing to hold on to, the counselor was able to help him move beyond the either-or thinking he was stuck in and see the complementary role that each could play in his recovery.
- Frieda arrived for her first session and announced that she'd taken an opiate pill just before coming in; prior to this she'd been clean for six weeks. Her counselor

helped her to recognize that she'd been anxious before the session, but initially Frieda could not identify the source of that anxiety, as she'd briefly been in counseling before and had been eager to resume. However, Frieda mentioned in passing that she knew that she must really "have the wind knocked out of her" in order to make progress in treatment.

When her counselor wondered where she'd gotten this idea, Frieda recounted an incident in rehab years before. A counselor had put great pressure on her to recall a painful event from early childhood. Though she had resisted, when she finally gave in and told the story, she experienced a searing pain in her chest, broke into tears, and then felt relieved. Since then Frieda assumed that all therapeutic progress required this kind of experience.

The counselor pointed out that the unintended consequence of her previous counselor's intervention had been to frighten her enough so that she now either avoided treatment or, as on that day, found ways to render it harmless. The counselor explained that such pressure was unnecessary and even counterproductive and reassured her that they could find ways of working on her problems that would not require her to go through similar experiences.

The Ending

The first motivational counseling session ends with the counselor once again taking an active structuring role. The counselor reviews the progress of the session and summarizes the central themes discussed and the moments of self-recognition the client experienced. Especially important to recall are self-motivational statements, goals, and plans.

CO: As I understand it, Teresa, you've become aware of a gradual increase in your marijuana use over the past

> year or so, to the point where you've been smoking pretty much every day. You've also been smoking while you were caring for your kids, which is something you'd told yourself you'd never do, and this started to worry you. You've also become aware that you've lost some of your drive. You don't clean the house as well as you used to, or get out as much, even though you always enjoyed that. You're not sure if you need to stop completely, and you think you'd miss the relaxation at times, but you're willing to try not to smoke at all for the next month, and for us to talk about how that's going and what changes you notice. You're also thinking about spending some special time with your kids and want to find some other ways to relax. Is that about it?

In ongoing sessions, the counselor would move from this summary into a confirmation of future arrangements. It is particularly important, if the counseling has a definite time or frequency structure, that the counselor remind the client of where they stand. In the first session, however, another piece is added in between the summary and the confirmation—a kind of *post-hoc structuring* to reorient the client, affirm the connection made with the counselor, and generally "close on good terms." This has four parts.

- Noting that the way they've been working together may be different from what was expected, the counselor asks the client how this session compared with his or her experiences in the hospital, rehab, or other outpatient treatments. Typically the client will be quite aware of these differences, and the counselor's explicit recognition of this is experienced as affirming.
- Summarizing the motivational counseling approach, the counselor states that the client is capable of his or her own decisions regarding change, emphasizes the importance of the client setting the agenda for the sessions, and describes the counselor's role as one of pro-

viding information, thinking with the client about his or her concerns, and helping the client achieve personal goals.

- Asking for the client's reaction to this approach, the counselor affirms self-motivational statements about continuing treatment, responds to questions, and remains nondefensive and interested in any doubts or concerns expressed.
- Conveying confidence in the approach, the counselor affirms the client's work in the session and expresses optimism about being able to help.

Following Up

The content of the follow-up sessions of motivational counseling will depend largely on the outcome of the first. Some clients will already have made or reaffirmed a clear commitment to change, in the form of abstinence from substances of abuse, faithful compliance with prescribed medications, regular attendance at self-help/support meetings, Twelve Step work, monitoring of negative thoughts, or any of the myriad other activities their recovery plan might comprise. For these clients, the counselor's goal in the ongoing sessions is to affirm their efforts and help them adjust their plan to meet changing needs. Other clients, of course, will be more hesitant and uncertain, and will express this through ambivalent statements and actions; in these cases, the counselor's goal is to continue to develop problem and treatment acceptance through the strategies and techniques we've already discussed.

The flexibility inherent in motivational counseling places greater demands on counselors than does the relatively predictable progression of more traditional approaches, but at the same time frees counselors to work in the orientation they are most comfortable with. Once clients have accepted the severity of the problem and the need for help in overcoming it—or, alternately, have reached the "action" stage and are well-engaged in treatment—they are likely to be amenable to whatever further form of help the counselor offers. This contention finds support in the one consistent finding in psychotherapy outcome research: that the quality of the relationship between counselor and client is the most accurate predictor of the success of the treatment, regardless of the counselor's orientation.[11]

There are nonetheless two key elements that may serve as anchors for the second motivational counseling session: the opening and the use of feedback.

The Opening

The purpose of the opening is, as before, to structure the session along the lines of the two desired foci (problem acceptance and treatment acceptance) while communicating that the client's concerns and agenda are of primary interest.

CO: We talked last time about a number of your concerns related to your marijuana use and your mood, Phillip. As I recall, you said that . . .

> *The counselor briefly summarizes the key points made by the client in the first session, emphasizing those associated with the client's perceptions of the significance of the problems, thoughts about change, and feelings about participating in treatment.*

I'm wondering whether you've had any further thoughts about this or taken any steps toward dealing with these issues.

This opening has a dual effect. It is open-ended enough to allow clients to respond at whatever levels of problem and treatment acceptance they find themselves at that moment. They can as easily answer "No, I haven't," as "Yes, I was thinking that I would . . ." It also conveys the message that the counselor is on top of things and interested in helping to resolve the client's concerns. From here on the dialogue will proceed in accordance with the client's active concerns and readiness to address them.

Feedback

As discussed in chapter 8, a central component of Miller's original Motivational Interviewing model was providing the client with personalized feedback of information gathered in an elaborate initial assessment. While it is possible to engage in motivational counseling without this, we have found a formal feedback process to be an excellent addition to the second session of our intervention. By this point, clients will in most cases have developed some sense of alliance with their counselor, enough so that discomforting information the counselor presents cannot be as easily brushed aside as it might have been before.

Counselors can choose from a wide variety of reliable instruments to assess the nature and consequences of clients' substance use or psychiatric disorders.[12] These can be integrated into the initial intake process and then summarized in a "feedback form" to be reviewed with the client.[13]

It is worth reemphasizing that feedback is not used by the motivational counselor to label clients, scare them, prove anything to them, or pressure them to change. Rather, it can help clients to recognize "where they are," and thus that they are not "where they want to be." In the course of the feedback session, the client's own reactions (verbal and nonverbal), feelings, and concerns are noticed, solicited, and reflected, and self-motivational statements are affirmed. If directly asked, the counselor may give an opinion about a particular result, but then immediately should ask for the client's thoughts or feelings about this opinion.[14]

Once the feedback has been provided, the counselor can

make an easy transition into a discussion of goals and whether these goals can be specified and clarified so they become the foundation for future work together. Important questions for the counselor to consider include: How does the client's current behavior, as revealed through the assessment tools, affect the client's ability to achieve important goals? What changes would be necessary for these goals to become achievable? These questions open up the topic of goals by putting the responsibility on the client to think them through and decide—with the counselor's assistance and appropriate advice—how to proceed.

The feedback section is the most structured portion of any motivational counseling session, and we have developed concrete guidelines for conducting it. These derive from Miller and Rollnick but also from the work of psychologist Constance Fischer, whose development of the process of "individualized assessment" has strongly influenced our current approach.[15]

Fischer provides the following important principles.

- Use everyday language, avoid jargon, and carefully explain any technical terms. *(When we talk about "dependence," what we mean is how much you've come to need a substance or how much you miss it when it's not there, either all the time or in particular situations, like work, or home, or out socializing.)*
- Give specific, concrete examples and explanations of the phenomena being described. *(Tolerance refers to taking in a large amount of a substance without showing the expected effects. Like when you smoked that "twenty" and didn't feel high at all.)*
- Treat life events and situations as primary. *(Last time you were telling me how, when you're high, you don't think much about who you're having sex with. That would make sense of this finding of your being at high risk for HIV infection.)*

- Take a collaborative approach. Engage the client as an active participant in understanding the client's problems as well as the client's capacity to deal with them.
- Expect that the client may not always agree on all the results; accept this as a natural facet of the divergence of perspectives rather than as a personal challenge. Where no consensus is finally possible, the counselor may simply "agree to disagree" with the client until further discussions allow resolution of the difference.
- Understand that assessment results are contextual, a portrait of the client from a given perspective; they are not "the whole Truth" about the client. This understanding discourages the belief that the counselor has the final say about the reality of the client's problems and situation. Such a belief tends to lead to the attitude that, if the client disagrees, he or she must be wrong; this attitude, in turn, tends to lead to an authoritarian stance that evokes argumentation and resistance from the client.
- Be aware that the client is not the same in all contexts. Finding out when and in what situations the client is *not* depressed, or *can* resist the urge to drink, opens up opportunities for supporting self-efficacy. Using this knowledge, the counselor can emphasize that the client is not hopelessly limited to a disordered way of living.

With these principles in mind, the counselor does the following:

- Introduces the use of feedback. *(You recall I mentioned at the end of our last session that we were going to look at some of the results of all those tests and questionnaires you completed.)*
- Affirms the client for participating. *(I know that there were a lot of them, and we appreciate the time you took. We're going to make good use of them today.)*

- Introduces and contextualizes the feedback form. *(Let me show you how we're going to do this. This is a summary of the results of the assessments you completed, and we're going to go through it together. I think that they will give us some important information about what things have been like for you and what's been happening in your life.)*
- Refers to the specific instrument that gave a particular result and reminds the client what it was like (self-report or assessor administered; types of questions, multiple choice, yes/no, etc.; example of questions asked).
- Explains what that instrument was attempting to assess (severity of depression, problems associated with drug use, involvement in behaviors that increase the risk of contracting HIV).
- Explains technical terms. *(By "depression" we mean experiencing such symptoms as feeling sad or irritable day after day, losing interest in the things you once enjoyed, having trouble eating or sleeping . . .)*
- Gives an overview of the scheme of measurement *(Scores can range from 0 to 70 depending on how often and how intensely you said those statements applied to you.)* and scoring norms *(0 to 10 is considered typical of people with no depression, 11 to 20 is associated with mild depression . . .).*
- Points out the client's score or result *(As you can see here, your score added up to 43 . . .)*, where it falls compared with norms *(. . . which puts you in the severe range of depression)*, and what this means in a broader sense to the client *(What this suggests is that you've been depressed enough so that it's probably been really hard for you to take care of things you'd normally take care of, maybe to the point where you found that you just weren't keeping up with things,*

and that life has been pretty miserable and joyless for you for a while now).

- Elicits the client's reaction *(How does this sound to you? Does it describe accurately what things have been like and how you've been feeling?)* and any life events and situations the assessment result helps make sense of *(Have there been times lately when you tried to keep up with things but ended up falling further behind?).*
- Reflects and summarizes the client's reactions, including what's accepted and what's doubted. *(As you think about it now, you really do see yourself as having been strongly affected by the depression we've been discussing, especially at times like the other day when you thought about going out and then decided against it, though you're not sure whether this is the way you've always been or if this is something new and different that you're dealing with.)*
- Makes a transition to the next result. *(So far we've been focusing mainly on how being depressed has been affecting your life; this next piece of information may tell us something important about how your cocaine use fits into the picture.)*
- Gives intermediate summaries. *(I think we've seen that not only has being depressed gotten in the way of taking care of things that are important to you but also getting high on a daily basis led you to give up on even trying to keep up. Let's see what else the results tell us.)*
- Summarizes the results and ensuing discussion, asks for reactions, and reflects ambivalences. *(So the assessments you completed suggested that both depression and cocaine use have interfered with your being able to take care of your family and yourself, and that the cocaine also has left you without money and*

vulnerable to contracting HIV through tricking in order for you to be able to afford to keep using. At the same time, you've got some mixed feelings about quitting though you're interested in talking with me about it. You're not so sure that you've been as depressed as the tests say you've been, though you know you haven't been yourself for a while. Is that about right?)

- Moves into a discussion of goals. *(One of the things you've come back to a couple of times is how important it is to you to be a better mother to your kids than you've been able to be recently. What are your thoughts about this now after looking together at these results?)*

Troubleshooting the Motivational Counseling Session: Possible Situations and Responses

The goal of motivational counseling is to reduce client resistance to problem and treatment acceptance. Counselors working in this style will find that the levels of resistance that they regularly encounter are lower than those they are accustomed to. Nonetheless, the counselor must be prepared for situations in which the client may seem to go off track or otherwise stray from the desired session foci. What follows is a review of common problem situations, and recommendations for how the motivational counselor might put things back on track.

Problem: *The client begins discussing issues unrelated to the substance abuse (and/or, if applicable, psychiatric) problem.*

Suggestions: *The counselor:*

- Explores the client's agenda until able to accurately summarize the concern and, if possible, the obstacles to resolving it.
- Frames this concern as something to work on together and emphasizes a wish to do so.
- Assesses (internally) the client's stage of change regarding this issue (*precontemplation,* i.e., sees it as others' problem; *contemplation,* i.e., considering the need for personal change; *preparation,* i.e., thinking about taking action; *action,* i.e., making a change).
- Asks: "Where do [drugs/alcohol]/[psychiatric disorder] fit in with this?"
- Reflects and explores client responses.

Problem: *A dual-disordered client talks* only *about substance use, or* only *about symptoms.*
Suggestions: *The counselor:*

- Explores the issue raised in depth, as above.
- Asks: "Where does [psychiatric disorder/substance] fit in with this?"
- Reflects and explores client responses.

Problem: *The client talks without focus or real interest about a particular area of his or her life.*
Suggestions: *The counselor:*

- Asks: "What concerns you the *most* about this?" or "What is the *worst* thing that could happen if you kept on going this way?"
- Reflects and explores client responses.

Problem: *The client talks noncommittally about a (possible) problem area.*
Suggestions: *The counselor:*

- Asks: "In what ways do you think you or other people have been harmed by ______?" "In what ways does this concern you?" "What do you think will happen if you don't make any changes in this area?"

- Assesses (internally) the client's level of interest/concern about this: if there is significant interest/concern, the counselor proceeds as above; if interest/concern is low, the counselor asks: "What area of your life is really concerning you right now?"

Problem: *The client talks as though he or she has no concerns or sees no problem areas.*
Suggestions: *The counselor:*

- States: "Your being here tells me that at least part of you has some concern about how things have been going. Could you fill me in about that part?"
- After reflection and elaboration, asks: "So ________ is a concern for you. What's the good side? What's the dark side?"

Problem: *The client continues to insist that he or she has no current concerns or worries.*
Suggestions: *The counselor:*

- Reflects the client's presentation in an amplified, or intensified, form:[16] "Right now, everything is going so well, there is nothing in your life that's concerning you."
- If the client affirms the most extreme statement of lack of concerns: reviews the client's history of struggles or past roadblocks encountered; asks about the purposes served by past problematic behavior, for example, "Looking back, what did [drugs/alcohol] do for you that seemed positive at the time?" "What did you like about [substance] when you first used?"
- Reviews the client's plans to meet these needs without substances.

- Reflects the importance to the client of believing that all will be OK.
- Inquires about the anxieties that might underlie this insistence: "What would it be like if you didn't succeed this time?"
- Empathically reflects these worries/fears.
- Suggests that by working together they can increase the client's chances of succeeding.

Problem: *The client claims having changed already/being "done."*
Suggestions: *The counselor:*

- Asks: "How have you achieved this change?"
- Explores discrepancies between the claimed change and the description of its achievement: "You've said that staying clean/keeping your mood positive isn't going to be difficult for you, and you've also told me that nothing has really changed as far as your situation is concerned and you aren't planning to do anything differently. Can you help me understand this?"
- Reflects and explores client responses.

Problem: *The client begins to talk about an area of life concern, but does not go beyond lamentations or expressions of hopelessness.*
Suggestions: *The counselor:*

- Asks: "What would you like to be different?" "When things were better, what were they like?" "What's different in this area than it used to be?" "Five years from now, what would you like your life to be like in this area?"
- Elaborates and explores life and instrumental goals.
- Identifies specific changes needed to achieve the goals.

- Affirms that the client *does* have some clear ideas about how life could be better or about what's important.
- Frames these as *life* or ultimate goals.
- Emphasizes that they can make progress in this area by working together on it.
- Asks about the key instrumental goals: "How do you see your substance use as relating to this?" "What effect do you think [substance] will have on your being able to make these changes?" "Does feeling depressed have an effect in this area?" "How would being anxious influence your being able to make things better?"
- Having explored the above, repeats the process with the substance/psychiatric problem as the goal, exploring the means to achieve it (instrumental goals).

Problem: *The client has frequently in the past endorsed goals without having made progress toward achieving them.*
Suggestions: *The counselor:*

- Asks: "What could help things be different this time?" "What seems different starting out this time?" "What might get in the way of accomplishing this?"
- Reflects and explores client responses.

Problem: *The client has changed behavior but continues to express ambivalent thoughts/feelings.*
Suggestions: *The counselor:*

- Normalizes recurring ambivalence.
- Explores feelings and concerns about maintaining change: What if I fail? How can I live without what I've given up? What if I can't do ________ anymore? What if I begin to feel overwhelmed?
- Reviews decisional balance (pros and cons of continuing change versus returning to previous behavior).

- Affirms self-motivational factors: goals being approached or reached, hopes for the future, optimism about maintaining change, past and current successes.

Compliance and Relapse in Early Recovery

One of the most common problem situations during the early period of treatment, and one that is among the greatest threats to treatment compliance, is the "slip" or brief return to substance use. Some clients will explicitly maintain nonabstinence goals, whatever the preference of the counselor. Episodes of use in such cases would not be considered "slips" and would be addressed by evaluating the effects and consequences of this course of action. Our focus here is on those clients who have committed to abstinence and maintained this for at least a brief period before resuming substance use.

We have found that this problem is best addressed from two vantage points. In some cases, a counselor may become aware—either because of client disclosure or because of other reliable indicators—that a client is teetering on the brink of returning to using but has not yet done so. In other cases, the counselor learns of this after the fact, when a client comes in and reports a slip.

Lapse Prevention: Reaffirming Commitment (The Case of Joseph)

When clients indicate, directly or indirectly, that they are considering resumption of substance use, the counselor's first reaction is likely to be disappointment, frustration, or anxiety. After all, the counselor may have been part of the hard work to achieve sobriety and may have clear ideas about what will happen if the client gives this up. Out of concern or other emotions, then, the counselor may try to argue or persuade the client out of this decision, bringing to bear the full force of the evidence regarding the value of abstinence.

The likely result, however, is just the opposite of what the counselor intends. Typically, the client will become defensive and manifest resistant behaviors similar to those of clients who are told they must make an immediate commitment to abstinence at the start of treatment.

Such client responses point toward the key issue in dealing with this situation: ambivalence. Though a client may have resolved ambivalence about change sufficiently to move into taking action and establishing sobriety, counselors must recognize that this resolution is rarely a permanent one the first time around. It is far more common for individuals who have made a major life decision to have second thoughts or doubts, or even to become convinced, at least briefly, that they have made the wrong decision, and to resolve to change their course of action. Of course, this is often a temporary condition, a reaction to the anxiety triggered by taking a step into the unknown. But sometimes the doubts are more persistent, or they return after a period of relative certainty when new factors enter into the equation.

The client considering a return to use, then, has returned to the contemplation stage of change, and the most effective intervention is likely to be one that fits the special needs of this stage. It might be useful to provide an extended clinical example of how such an intervention might work.

Joseph, a young man in his early twenties, carried the diagnoses of alcohol dependence, cocaine abuse, dysthymia, and adult attention deficit hyperactivity disorder (ADHD). At the time of this episode he and his counselor had been working together for just a few weeks, but Joseph had been abstinent from all substances for almost eight months. Joseph described a chaotic adolescence during which he progressed from occasional drinking with friends to getting wasted three or four times a week, running afoul of the juvenile authorities, and missing school. He eventually dropped out and spent his time on the street corner drinking jug wine and panhandling money to buy cocaine, which he felt improved his ability to think clearly. This lasted until the day when, after falling down drunk in front of a girl he was trying to flirt with, he swore he'd quit drinking, and he did so.

After establishing that Joseph was actively maintaining his abstinence, the counselor focused treatment on the difficulties Joseph had had for many years with concentration, task persistence, and the like. The young man revealed that he had always struggled in school despite being told he had above-average intelligence, and he told the counselor that he wanted to learn how to make more of his life than he had so far.

In an early session, Joseph mentioned in passing that he'd been wondering lately whether it might be OK for him to sign up for a wine-tasting course being offered at the local community college. He dismissed the idea as quickly as he'd brought it up, however, and little was said other than the counselor's suggestion that they talk about such ideas if and when they arise.

The following week Joseph again brought up the wine-tasting course and this time said he was seriously considering signing up. He'd always been interested in the "finer things" in life (he'd heard that wine could be one of them) and he wasn't sure he wanted to deny himself the opportunity to learn about it in a sophisticated way. He wanted to know how this would affect the medication he was taking for his ADHD.

The counselor immediately thought of how easily Joseph could slip from "tasting" to "guzzling," and naturally was concerned about the possibility that Joseph would lose what he had been working so hard to accomplish over the past year. The counselor also knew, however, that to bring up these thoughts to Joseph meant losing contact with where he was at that moment, and thus probably engendering resentment and possibly withdrawal. Instead, the counselor responded as follows.

> CO: It sounds as though this is something you've been giving a lot of thought to. I think it would be useful for us to talk about the decision you're trying to make. As far as the medication is concerned, there are risks to mixing it with alcohol, and I'm sure your doctor would strongly advise you not to do so. Still, I'm not going to tell you what to do about this, since it really is your decision and you're the only one who can make it. What I'm wondering is, what are some of the reasons you think you'd like to try this wine-tasting course?

Joseph responded initially by repeating his wish to become more familiar with the finer things in life, saying he saw the course as an easily available (and relatively cheap) way of achieving his goal. The counselor reflected this back, then asked whether there might be other positives as well in making this choice. Joseph then spoke of his new girlfriend, a social drinker who liked to share a bottle of wine at dinner. She knew about his problems and had refrained from serving wine with meals. Now Joseph felt as though he was denying her this pleasure unfairly. He thought that, if he could restrict his drinking to a glass or two of wine at meals, then they could both be satisfied.

> CO: At least a couple of things are on the side of taking the course. You really would like to gain some sophistication, and this could be a way of doing that without breaking the bank. You've also been feeling bad about not being able to join your girlfriend in a bottle of wine over dinner, maybe wondering if she might feel deprived of something she enjoys. She's been very consid-

erate of your needs, and you want to be considerate of hers. Is that about it?

Joseph went on to elaborate on both of these reasons. His ideas of "sophistication" came from a favorite uncle whom he'd always looked up to. This uncle had been something of a wine connoisseur, and Joseph had fantasized since he was a kid about going into a restaurant and knowing exactly which wine to order to impress his date. He also worried that his girlfriend might become resentful in time about being so restricted due to his alcohol problems, and he thought drinking wine occasionally might be a way of preventing this.

CO: So these are some pretty significant concerns about giving up the option of trying to drink in a controlled way. What else?

CL: It's not just for my girlfriend. When I see other couples in restaurants having dinner, drinking wine, it all just looks so *normal*. I mean, why can't I do normal things like other people, you know? Am I going to have to be restricted everywhere I turn just because I had some problems for a while?

CO: When you think about not being able to do what other people do, you really feel frustrated and angry about that. It's like you're an alien, you don't belong with other people, and even worse, like maybe there's something wrong with you and you're being punished for it.

Joseph resonated deeply with the connection of his feelings of frustration with a sense of being punished. He talked about how he'd always gotten into trouble in school because he couldn't sit still, then ending up in the remedial class or, as he put it, "the class for us dumb kids."

CL: I always felt like there was something wrong with me, you know, that made me not be able to be with the "normal" kids. I guess there's a little of that feeling when I think about not being able to drink like other people anymore.

At this point the counselor had drawn out most of what was important to Joseph about trying to drink in a limited way. Nonetheless, the counselor wanted to be sure.

CO: Is there anything else in favor of taking this course?

In response to this question, Joseph looked a bit sheepish.

CL: Well, I guess I did kind of miss that warm feeling when the wine hits your throat, and then that moment of feeling good in your head when it gets there. I guess I was thinking that it would be nice to have that again, just a little bit, where I couldn't get too out of hand.

Many counselors might assume that, finally, Joseph had gotten to the "real" reason for taking the course—wanting to get buzzed. In contrast, his counselor was convinced that *all* of his reasons were significant and played a role in his decision. After all, if he could catch a mild buzz, feel sophisticated and at the same time like one of the crowd, and ensure his girlfriend's love all at the same time, why *wouldn't* the wine course appeal to him?

By this time the end of the session was approaching.

CO: Joseph, we've been talking about all the positive things about taking this course, and it's clear that you have a lot of reasons for wanting to. At the same time, I think there's also another side to the story, which is why you brought it up to talk about with me. What I'd like to suggest is this: that you defer your decision about the wine course until we've had the chance to look together at both sides. At that point you'll make your own decision, either to take the course or to reaffirm your commitment to abstinence. How does that sound?

CL: That sounds good. I actually like the idea of talking

about this. You know, when I went into detox I did it really without thinking about abstinence much, basically because it looked like the only way out. And the truth is, I really haven't thought about it until now. Maybe it's time I did.

The counselor was not sure, as the session ended, that this approach would be effective and wondered if Joseph would go ahead and sign up or whether he would even come back to talk about it. He did come back the next week, but spoke for most of the session about a series of problems he'd been having with his girlfriend. At first, the counselor saw this as obvious avoidance, and was prepared to break in and redirect him to the previous discussion. He soon realized, however, that the conflicts Joseph was describing were exactly parallel to those he had about the wine course. Sometimes he felt as though his girlfriend saw him as "abnormal" because of his checkered history and may even have been embarrassed to be with him. When she would tell him she couldn't see him on a particular day, he'd wonder if she was mad at him and punishing him, and would start to put himself down (or "punish" himself) for not being good enough for her. Lately he'd been thinking they should break up because he didn't think he "needed the aggravation."

Much of the session was spent exploring these conflicts. The counselor then made the connection with their earlier concern.

CO: You told me earlier that you and Tiffany got together kind of suddenly.

CL: Yeah, we met at a party three months ago after I broke up with my old girlfriend, and the next day we started going out.

CO: You know, I'm thinking that there's an interesting similarity between how you decided to get involved with her, and how you decided to stop drinking. Both were kind of impulsive decisions, and both came when you were hurting and saw a quick way to ease that hurt. I wonder if it wouldn't be useful for us to look at your relationship with Tiffany the same way as we started to look at your decision about the wine course—really examine both sides so you can decide what you want to do about it.

CL: Yeah. I guess that would help. But we don't need to do that about the course. I thought about it after last time, and I realized that none of those reasons were good enough to risk ending up where I was before I went into detox. I really like being more stable and the course isn't that important. I can always become an art connoisseur instead. (*Laughing*)

By joining with Joseph's wish to acknowledge the good things about drinking—the things he missed—the counselor prevented a battle in which Joseph would feel compelled to defend himself. Instead, the effect was to increase their alliance while also encouraging Joseph to think through an important decision and make it himself—a process that ran counter to, and thus was a corrective experience for, his problems of attention and impulsivity. Joseph demonstrated that clients will often do the work themselves—as counselors wish them to do—if they are given the autonomy they are seeking.

Further, the message implied by the counselor's stance—that the counselor, as a figure of authority, would not punish Joseph for his "out of line" thoughts or behavior, but would try to understand them from his perspective—was itself a source of healing. They were, in fact, later able to look at his relationship decision together, help him resolve it to his satisfaction, and continue to work together profitably. Joseph remained sober when they completed their work several months later.

Lapse Management: Reestablishing Commitment

It is not possible, of course, to head off in every instance the client's resumption of substance use. In some cases, a client's return to substance use happens unpredictably and without warning. In others, clients find themselves attempting to use in a way that will avoid the severe negative consequences experienced before. Where the client has made a clear choice to try using again, the counselor's role is not to argue with that choice but to help the client recognize and evaluate its consequences. In most instances, though, the decision to use will have been an impulsive one or one made under pressure of strong urges or cravings, and clients will not experience themselves as having really made a decision so much as succumbed to temptation.

The client is likely to experience such an episode of use as a *failure,*[17] and to anticipate that the counselor will view it the same way. Therefore the counselor's response to learning that the client has used after a period of abstinence can do much to increase or decrease the client's sense of self-efficacy and motivation to continue in treatment.

The motivational counselor follows guidelines compatible with Relapse Prevention approaches[18] but does so in the distinctive style of motivational counseling. The most important guideline is to recognize that the client's return to a session after an incident of using is, in fact, a *success*. It represents a change from a past pattern of using for long periods and abandoning responsibilities and commitments while doing so. The return also may signify a high degree of alliance with the counselor, a willingness to risk the condemnation the client fears to receive the understanding welcome the client craves. The counselor's willingness to verbalize these ideas may go a long way toward supporting the client's efforts to reestablish abstinence.

Once this overall understanding has been communicated, the counselor can proceed with a semistructured intervention designed to help the client reestablish commitment to change. The counselor suggests to the client that it would be useful to look together at the episode of use, naming it as a "lapse" to distinguish it from a "collapse" or complete relapse, and notes that by doing so they can turn this moment of disappointment into a learning experience that may help the client to achieve greater success in the future. It is important that the counselor does not insist on doing this, but offers it as an option and affirms the client's willingness to do this work together.

The counselor then asks the client about his or her perceptions of the incident; and, if perceptions or concerns are offered, these are drawn out and elaborated on. Special attention is given to any ambivalence expressed by the client regarding a return to substance use, and the pros and cons of abstinence versus getting high may be reviewed, as well as obstacles the client perceives to achieving his or her goals. If the client is receptive to further discussion, the counselor suggests a detailed review of the incident and the events leading to it. Once again the client is affirmed if willing to continue; if not, the counselor returns to the client's pressing concerns.

In cases where the client is indeed receptive, the counselor engages in what has been termed a "relapse debriefing."[19] This involves a review of the chain of events leading to incident of use, with the goal of identifying a number of important factors typically associated with such lapses: high-risk situations and factors; decision points along the way (overt and those that seem irrelevant); warning signs that could be recognized in future such situations; coping strategies used by the client and where they fell short.

As the review ends, the counselor summarizes the concerns and perceptions expressed by the client, the counselor's own observations and concerns, and the goals the client is committed to as well as the obstacles that have been identified. This is followed by a "key question"[20]—"What about next time?" "How do you plan to deal with this in the future?"—and then an effort at planning for future occurrences. As always, the counselor first invites the client to offer options for relapse prevention and these are discussed and evaluated together. If the client is receptive, the counselor may offer strategies specific to the client. The client's reactions, perceptions of obstacles, and other concerns are then discussed, after which the counselor explicitly asks for commitment to the plan: "Do you feel ready? Will this work for you?"

If the client hesitates, the counselor may have moved too fast and may want to return to summarizing what has been discussed and asking the client for further thoughts and concerns. If the client agrees, the counselor again affirms his or her participation in the discussion, summarizes the evidence that the client is capable of carrying this plan through, and invites further discussions of similar incidents should they arise. The focus of the session, if time remains, can then shift to the client's other current concerns.

Conclusion

It is clear from clinical experience and numerous research studies that much can be done to improve compliance among clients with substance use disorders, including those with additional psychiatric disorders. A comprehensive approach to improving compliance looks at this issue from several perspectives: client; family and social environment; counselor, therapist, or other caregiver; and treatment program or agency. In this book, we have provided a multiplicity of compliance-enhancing interventions that take into consideration each of these perspectives. We feel strongly that implementing these interventions will improve compliance behaviors among clients. This, in turn, will improve clinical outcome. Clearly, any improvement counselors and treatment agencies make regarding the compliance of the clients they serve has many potential benefits to clients, their families, treatment agencies, counselors, and insurance companies. We need to continue exploring new ways of addressing this age-old problem of poor compliance.

Notes

Chapter 1

Introduction and Overview

1. L. N. Robins and D. A. Regier, eds., *Psychiatric Disorders in America: The Epidemiologic Catchment Area Study* (New York: Free Press, 1991).
2. The following research monograph, recently published by the National Institute on Drug Abuse, contains ten papers that summarize much of the research on compliance, retention, and treatment outcome related to various types of drug abuse: L. Simon-Onken, J. D. Blaine, and J. J. Boren, eds., "Beyond the Therapeutic Alliance: Keeping the Drug-Dependent Individual in Treatment," *National Institute on Drug Abuse Monograph 165* (Rockville, Md.: U.S. Department of Health and Human Services, 1997).
3. M. D. Mueller and J. R. Wyman, "Study Sheds New Light on the State of Drug Abuse Treatment Nationwide," *NIDA Notes* 12, no. 5 (September/October 1997).
4. K. M. Carroll, "Enhancing Retention in Clinical Trials of Psychosocial Treatments: Practical Strategies," *in* L. Simon-Onken, J. D. Blaine, and J. J. Boren, eds., "Beyond the Therapeutic Alliance: Keeping the Drug-Dependent Individual in Treatment," *National Institute on Drug Abuse Monograph 165* (Rockville, Md.: U.S. Department of Health and Human Services, 1997): 4–24.
5. D. C. Daley et al., "Increasing Treatment Adherence Among Outpatients with Depression and Cocaine Dependence: Results of a Pilot Study," *American Journal of Psychiatry* 155 (1998): 1611–13; D. C. Daley and A. Zuckoff, "Improving Compliance with the Initial Outpatient Session Among Discharged Inpatient Dual Diagnosis Clients," *Social Work* 43, no. 5 (1998): 470–73.

Chapter 2

Types of Compliance Problems

1. D. S. Festinger et al., "Pretreatment Dropout as a Function of Treatment Delay and Client Variables," *Addictive Behaviors* 20, no. 1 (1995): 111–15; J. Garrett et al., "ARISE: A Method for Engaging Reluctant Alcohol- and Drug-Dependent Individuals in Treatment," *Journal of Substance Abuse Treatment* 14, no. 3 (1997): 235–48; Y. Hser et al., "Predicting Drug Treatment Entry Among Treatment-

Seeking Individuals," *Journal of Substance Abuse Treatment* 15, no. 3 (1998): 213–20; D. R. Orme and D. Boswell, "The Pre-Intake Drop-Out at a Community Mental Health Center," *Community Mental Health Journal* 27, no. 5 (1991): 375–79; D. D. Simpson et al., "Client Engagement and Change During Abuse Treatment," *Journal of Substance Abuse* 7 (1995): 117–34; B. Thom et al., "Engaging Patients with Alcohol Problems in Treatment: The First Consultation," *British Journal of Addiction* 87 (1992): 601–11.

2. We tracked several hundred referrals and found that patients with cocaine use disorders and patients initially treated on an inpatient unit had the lowest compliance rates with the initial outpatient evaluation.
3. T. W. Haywood et al., "Predicting the 'Revolving Door' Phenomenon Among Patients with Schizophrenic, Schizoaffective, and Affective Disorders," *American Journal of Psychiatry* 152, no. 6 (1995): 856–61; J. S. Verinis and J. Taylor, "Increasing Alcoholic Patients' Aftercare Attendance," *The International Journal of Addictions* 29, no. 11 (1994): 1487–94; P. R. Wolpe et al., "Predicting Compliance of Dual Diagnosis Inpatients with Aftercare Treatment," *Hospital and Community Psychiatry* 44, no. 1 (1993): 45–49; Festinger et al., "Pretreatment Dropout as a Function of Treatment Delay and Client Variables," 111–15; S. J. Lash, "Increasing Participation in Substance Abuse Aftercare Treatment," *American Journal of Drug and Alcohol Abuse* 24, no. 1 (1998): 31–36; J. R. McKay et al., "Predictors of Participation in Aftercare Sessions and Self-Help Groups Following Completion of Intensive Outpatient Treatment for Substance Abuse," *Journal of Studies on Alcohol* 59 (1998): 152–62; P. Solomon, "Receipt of Aftercare Services by Problem Types: Psychiatric, Psychiatric/Substance Abuse and Substance Abuse," *Psychiatric Quarterly* 58, no. 3 (fall 1986–87): 180–88; K. Tomasson and P. Vaglum, "Psychiatric Co-morbidity and Aftercare Among Alcoholics: A Prospective Study of a Nationwide Representative Sample," *Addiction* 93, no. 3 (1998): 423–31; M. D. Carpenter et al., "Multiple Admissions to an Urban Psychiatric Center: A Comparative Study," *Hospital and Community Psychiatry* 36, no. 12 (1985): 1305–08; E. S. Casper, J. M. Romo, and R. C. Fasnacht, "Readmission Patterns of Frequent Users of Inpatient Psychiatric Services," *Hospital and Community Psychiatry* 42, no. 11 (1991): 1166–69; E. S. Casper and B. Donaldson, "Subgroups in the Population of Frequent Users of Inpatient Services," *Hospital and Community Psychiatry* 41, no. 2 (1990): 189–91; J. L. Geller, "In Again, Out Again: Preliminary Evaluation of a State Hospital's Worst Recidivists," *Hospital and Community Psychiatry* 37, no. 4 (1986): 386–90; W. A. Goodpastor and B. K. Hare, "Factors Associated with Multiple Readmissions to an Urban Public Psychiatric Hospital," *Hospital and Community Psychiatry* 42, no. 1 (1991): 85–87; J. H. Green, "Frequent Rehospitalization and Noncompliance with Treatment," *Hospital and Community Psychiatry* 39, no. 9 (1988): 963–66; J. W. Hull et al., "Factors Associated with Multiple Hospitalizations of Patients with Borderline Personality

Disorder," *Psychiatric Services* 47, no. 6 (1996): 638–41; T. Lewis and P. R. Joyce, "The New Revolving-Door Patients: Results from a National Cohort of First Admissions," *ACTA Psychiatric Scandanavia* 82 (1990): 130–35; R. H. Moos and B. S. Moos, "Stay in Residential Facilities and Mental Health Care as Predictors of Readmission for Patients with Substance Use Disorders," *Psychiatric Services* 46, no. 1 (1995): 66–72; C. Owen et al., "Psychiatric Rehospitalization Following Hospital Discharge," *Community Mental Health Journal* 33, no. 1 (1997): 13–22; R.W. Surber et al., "Characteristics of High Users of Acute Psychiatric Inpatient Services," *Hospital and Community Psychiatry* 38, no. 10 (1987): 1112–14; R. E. Drake et al., "The Course, Treatment, and Outcome of Substance Disorder in Persons with Severe Mental Illness," *American Journal of Orthopsychiatry* 66, no. 1 (1996): 42–51; C. R. Miner et al., "Prediction of Compliance with Outpatient Referral in Patients with Schizophrenia and Psychoactive Substance Use Disorders," *Archives of General Psychiatry* 54 (1997): 706–12; L. Olfson et al., "Linking Inpatients with Schizophrenia to Outpatient Care," *Psychiatric Services* 49, no. 7 (1988): 911–17; C. Owen et al., "Noncompliance in Psychiatric Aftercare," *Community Mental Health Journal* 33, no. 1 (1997): 25–34.

4. A. I. Alterman et al., "Prediction of Attrition from Day Hospital Treatment in Lower Socioeconomic Cocaine-Dependent Men," *Drug and Alcohol Dependence* 40 (1996): 227–33; J. E. Berg and J. I. Brevik, "Complaints That Predict Drop-Out from a Detoxification and Counseling Unit," *Addictive Behaviors* 23, no. 1 (1998): 35–40; D. A. Brizer, R. Maslansky, and M. Galanter, "Treatment Retention of Patients Referred by Public Assistance to an Alcoholism Clinic," *American Journal of Drug and Alcohol Abuse* 16, nos. 3 & 4 (1990): 259–64; W. S. Condelli and G. De Leon, "Fixed and Dynamic Predictors of Client Retention in Therapeutic Communities," *Journal of Substance Abuse Treatment* 10 (1993): 11–16; R. Castaneda, H. Lifshutz, and M. Galanter, "Treatment Compliance after Detoxification among Highly Disadvantaged Alcoholics," *American Journal of Drug and Alcohol Abuse* 18, no. 2 (1992): 223–34; G. Leigh, A. C. Ogborne, and P. Cleland, "Factors Associated with Patient Dropout from an Outpatient Alcoholism Treatment Service," *Journal of Studies on Alcohol* 45, no. 4 (1984): 359–62; J. Louks, J. Mason, and F. Backus, "AMA Discharges: Prediction and Treatment Outcome," *Hospital and Community Psychiatry* 40, no. 3 (1989): 299–301; N. E. Noel et al., "Predictors of Attrition from an Outpatient Alcoholism Treatment Program for Couples," *Journal of Studies on Alcohol* 48, no. 3 (1987): 229–35; J. S. Verinis, "Characteristics of Patients Who Continue with Alcohol Outpatient Treatment," *The International Journal of the Addictions* 21, no. 1 (1986): 25–31.

5. D. C. Daley et al., "Increasing Treatment Adherence Among Outpatients with Depression and Cocaine Dependence: Results of a Pilot Study," *American Journal of Psychiatry* 155 (1998): 1611–13.

6. V. Agosti et al., "Patient Factors Related to Early Attrition from an Outpatient Cocaine Research Clinic: A Preliminary Report," *The International Journal of the Addictions* 26, no. 3 (1991): 327–34; R. R. Gainey et al., "Predicting Treatment Retention among Cocaine Users," *The International Journal of the Addictions* 28, no. 5 (1993): 487–505; J. A. Hoffman et al., "Comparative Cocaine Abuse Treatment Strategies: Enhancing Client Retention and Treatment Exposure," *Experimental Therapeutics in Addiction Medicine* 13, no. 4 (1994): 115–28; L. M. Najavits and R. D. Weiss, "The Role of Psychotherapy in the Treatment of Substance Use Disorder," *Harvard Review of Psychiatry* 2 (1994): 84–86; S. Y. Kang et al., "Outcomes for Cocaine Abusers after One-A-Week Psychosocial Therapy," *American Journal of Psychiatry* 148 (1991): 630–35; Gainey et al., "Predicting Treatment Retention Among Cocaine Users," 487–505; P. H. Kleinman et al., "Retention of Cocaine Abusers in Outpatient Psychotherapy," *American Journal of Drug and Alcohol Abuse* 18, no. 1 (1992): 29–43; R. C. McMahon and A. Kelley, "Personality and Coping Styles in the Prediction of Dropout from Treatment for Cocaine Abuse," *Journal of Personality Assessment* 61, no. 1 (1993): 147–55.
7. T. A. Eckman et al., "Teaching Medication Management Skills to Schizophrenic Patients," *Journal of Clinical Psychopharmacology* 10, no. 1 (1990): 33–38; M. J. Goldstein, "Psychosocial Strategies for Maximizing the Effects of Psychotropic Medications for Schizophrenia and Mood Disorder," *Psychopharmacology Bulletin* 28, no. 3 (1992): 237–40; D. H. Fram, J. Marmo, and R. Holden, "Naltrexone Treatment: The Problem of Patient Acceptance," *Journal of Substance Abuse Treatment* 6 (1989): 119–22; S. G. Adams and J. T. Howe, "Predicting Medication Compliance in a Psychotic Population," *The Journal of Nervous and Mental Disease* 181 (1993): 558–60; E. Frank, D. J. Kupfer, and L. R. Siegel, "Alliance Not Compliance: A Philosophy of Outpatient Care," *Journal of Clinical Psychiatry* 56, suppl. 1 (1995): 11–17; C. A. Pristach and C. M. Smith, "Medication Compliance and Substance Abuse Among Schizophrenic Patients," *Hospital and Community Psychiatry* 41, no. 12 (1990): 1345–48; L. J. Heyduk, "Medication Education: Increasing Patient Compliance," *Journal of Psychosocial Nursing* 29, no. 12 (1991): 32–35.

Chapter 3
Factors Affecting Client Compliance

1. M. J. Stark, "Dropping Out of Substance Abuse Treatment: A Clinically Oriented Review," *Clinical Psychology Review* 12 (1992): 93–116; S. J. Bartels, R. E. Drake, and M. A. Wallach, "Long-Term Course of Substance Use Disorders Among Patients with Severe Mental Illness," *Psychiatric Services* 46, no. 3 (1995): 248–51; B. E. Havassy and P. G. Arns, "Relationship of Cocaine and Other Substance Dependence to Well-Being of High-Risk Psychiatric Patients," *Psychiatric Services* 49, no. 7

(1998): 935–40; D. A. Krulee and R. E. Hales, "Compliance with Psychiatric Referrals from a General Hospital Psychiatry Outcome Clinic," *General Hospital Psychiatry* 10 (1988): 339–45; J. Westermeyer, "Nontreatment Factors Affecting Treatment Outcome in Substance Abuse," *American Journal of Drug and Alcohol Abuse* 15, no. 1 (1989): 13–29; R. Walker et al., "High-Risk Factors for Rehospitalization Within Six Months," *Psychiatric Quarterly* 67, no. 3 (1996): 235–42; S. Kent and P. Yellowlees, "Psychiatric and Social Reasons for Frequent Rehospitalization," *Hospital and Community Psychiatry* 45, no. 4 (1994): 347–50; C. Sweet, "Symptom Severity and Number of Previous Psychiatric Admissions as Predictors of Readmission," *Psychiatric Services* 46, no. 6 (1995): 482–85; A. Chen, "Noncompliance in Community Psychiatry: A Review of Clinical Interventions," *Hospital and Community Psychiatry* 42, no. 3 (1991): 282–87; P. Solomon and B. Gordon, "Outpatient Compliance of Psychiatric Emergency Room Patients by Presenting Problems," *Psychiatric Quarterly* 59, no. 4 (1988): 271–83; T. T. H. Wan and Y. A. Ozcan, "Determinants of Psychiatric Rehospitalization: A Social Area Analysis," *Community Mental Health Journal* 27, no. 1 (1991): 3–16.

2. G. A. Marlatt, "Help-Seeking by Substance Abusers: The Role of Harm Reduction and Behavioral-Economic Approaches to Facilitate Treatment Entry and Retention," *in* L. Simon-Onken, J. D. Blaine, and J. J. Boren, eds., "Beyond the Therapeutic Alliance: Keeping the Drug-Dependent Individual in Treatment," *National Institute on Drug Abuse Monograph 165* (Rockville, Md.: U.S. Department of Health and Human Services, 1997): 44–84.
3. K. Tomasson and P. Vaglum, "The 2 Year Course Following Detoxification Treatment of Substance Abuse: The Possible Influence of Psychiatric Comorbidity," *European Archives of Psychiatry & Clinical Neuroscience* 247, no. 6 (1997): 320–27; S. J. Lash and W. Dillard, "Encouraging Participation in Aftercare Group Therapy Among Substance-Dependent Men," *Psychological Reports* 79, no. 2 (1996): 585–86; S. L. Lash, "Increasing Participation in Substance Abuse Aftercare Treatment," *American Journal of Drug and Alcohol Abuse* 24, no. 1 (1998): 31–36; L. T. Postrado and A. F. Lehman, "Quality of Life and Clinical Predictors of Rehospitalization of Persons with Severe Mental Illness," *Psychiatric Services* 26, no. 11 (1995): 1161–65; C. J. Bradley and G. A. Zarkin, "Inpatient Stays for Patients Diagnosed with Severe Psychiatric Disorders and Substance Abuse," *Health Services Research* 31, no. 4 (1996): 387–408; J. H. Green, "Frequent Rehospitalization and Noncompliance with Treatment," *Hospital and Community Psychiatry* 39, no. 9 (1988): 963–66.
4. G. E. Woody et al., "Sociopathy and Psychotherapy Outcome," *Archives of General Psychiatry* 42 (1985): 1081–86; L. Luborsky et al., "Therapist Success and Its Determinants," *Archives of General Psychiatry* 42 (1985): 602–11; L. Gerstley et al., "Ability to Form an Alliance with the Therapist: A Possible Marker of Prognosis for Patients with Antisocial Personality Disorder," *American Journal of Psychiatry* 146, no. 4 (1989): 508–12.

5. D. S. Festinger et al., "Pretreatment Dropout as a Function of Treatment Delay and Client Variables," *Addictive Behaviors* 20, no. 1 (1995): 111–15; M. Matas, D. Staley, and Wilman Griffin, "A Profile of the Noncompliant Patient: A Thirty-Month Review of Outpatient Psychiatry Referrals," *General Hospital Psychiatry* 14 (1992): 124–30.
6. Project MATCH Research Group, "Matching Alcoholism Treatments to Client Heterogeneity: Project MATCH Posttreatment Drinking Outcomes," *Journal of Studies on Alcohol* 58 (1997): 7–29; W. R. Miller et al., "What Works? A Methodological Analysis of the Alcohol Treatment Outcome Literature," *in* R. K. Hester and W. R. Miller, eds., *Handbook of Alcoholism Treatment Approaches: Effective Alternatives,* 2d ed. (Needham Heights, Mass.: Allyn and Bacon, 1995): 12–44.
7. L. Simon-Onken and J. D. Blaine, "Psychotherapy and Counseling in the Treatment of Drug Abuse," *National Institute on Drug Abuse Monograph 104* (Rockville, Md.: U.S. Department of Health and Human Services, 1990).

Chapter 4
Effects of Compliance Problems

1. M. J. Stark, "Dropping Out of Substance Abuse Treatment: A Clinically Oriented Review," *Clinical Psychology Review* 12 (1992): 93–116.
2. This was conducted as a quality assurance/quality improvement study that focused on patients' reasons for their psychiatric rehospitalization. A recurrent theme we hear among clients is that failure to comply with outpatient treatment (therapy and/or medications) often leads to symptom exacerbation, which, in turn, contributes to rehospitalization.
3. This was conducted as a quality assurance/quality improvement study. We looked simply at the rates of psychiatric rehospitalization between patients who complied with and those who failed to comply with their referral to outpatient/aftercare. Those who failed to comply with their referral were five times more likely to be rehospitalized compared with those who complied. While this was not a systematic study and other factors certainly could have contributed to rehospitalization, failure to comply with outpatient care appears to raise the relative risk of rehospitalization.
4. D. C. Daley et al., "Increasing Treatment Adherence Among Outpatients with Depression and Cocaine Dependence: Results of a Pilot Study," *American Journal of Psychiatry* 155 (1998): 1611-13.
5. T. W. Haywood et al., "Predicting the 'Revolving Door' Phenomenon Among Patients with Schizophrenic, Schizoaffective, and Affective Disorders," *American Journal of Psychiatry* 152, no. 6 (1995): 856–61; P. Solomon, "Receipt of Aftercare Services by Problem Types: Psychiatric, Psychiatric/Substance Abuse and Substance Abuse," *Psychiatric Quarterly* 58, no. 3 (fall 1986–87): 180–88; M. D. Carpenter et al., "Multiple Admissions to an Urban Psychiatric Center: A Comparative Study,"

Hospital and Community Psychiatry 36, no. 12 (1985): 1305–08; E. S. Casper, J. M. Romo, and R. C. Fasnacht, "Readmission Patterns of Frequent Users of Inpatient Psychiatric Services," *Hospital and Community Psychiatry* 42, no. 11 (1991): 1166–69; E. Casper and B. Donaldson, "Subgroups in the Population of Frequent Users of Inpatient Services," *Hospital and Community Psychiatry* 41, no. 2 (1990): 189–91; J. L. Geller, "In Again, Out Again: Preliminary Evaluation of a State Hospital's Worst Recidivists," *Hospital and Community Psychiatry* 37, no. 4 (1986): 386–90; W. A. Goodpastor and B. K. Hare, "Factors Associated with Multiple Readmissions to an Urban Public Psychiatric Hospital," *Hospital and Community Psychiatry* 42, no. 1 (1991): 85–87; J. W. Hull et al., "Factors Associated with Multiple Hospitalizations of Patients with Borderline Personality Disorder," *Psychiatric Services* 47, no. 6 (1996): 638–41; T. Lewis and P. R. Joyce, "The New Revolving-Door Patients: Results from a National Cohort of First Admissions," *ACTA Psychiatric Scandanavia* 82 (1990): 130–35; R. H. Moos and B. S. Moos, "Stay in Residential Facilities and Mental Health Care as Predictors of Readmission for Patients with Substance Use Disorders," *Psychiatric Services* 46, no. 1 (1995): 66–72; C. Owen et al., "Psychiatric Rehospitalization Following Hospital Discharge," *Community Mental Health Journal* 33, no. 1 (1997): 13-22; R. W. Surber et al., "Characteristics of High Users of Acute Psychiatric Inpatient Services," *Hospital and Community Psychiatry* 38, no. 10 (1987): 1112–14.

6. D. C. Daley and M. S. Raskin, *Treating the Chemically Dependent and Their Families* (Newbury Park, Calif.: Sage, 1991); D. C. Daley, H. B. Moss, and F. Campbell, *Dual Disorders: Counseling Clients with Chemical Dependency and Mental Illness* (Center City, Minn.: Hazelden, 1993), 45–60; D. C. Daley and I. M. Salloum, "The Family Factor," *Professional Counselor* (August 1996): 51–54; D. C. Daley and I. M. Salloum, "Focusing on Dual Disorders," *Professional Counselor* (October 1995): 15–26; R. E. Clark, "Family Costs Associated with Severe Mental Illness and Substance Use," *Hospital and Community Psychiatry* 45, no. 8 (1994): 808–13; C. Janzen, "Family Treatment for Alcoholism: A Review," *Social Work* (March 1978): 135–41; E. Kaufman, "Family Systems and Family Therapy of Substance Abuse: An Overview of Two Decades of Research and Clinical Experience," *The International Journal of the Addictions* 20, nos. 6 & 7 (1985): 897–916; R. L. Collins, K. E. Leonard, and J. S. Searles, eds., *Alcohol and the Family: Research and Clinical Perspectives* (New York: Guilford Press, 1990); M. D. Stanton and A. W. Heath, "Family and Marital Therapy," in J. H. Lowinson et al., eds., *Substance Abuse: A Comprehensive Textbook*, 3d ed. (Baltimore: Williams & Wilkins, 1997): 448–54.

Chapter 5

Counseling Strategies to Improve Compliance

1. M. J. Stark, "Dropping Out of Substance Abuse Treatment: A Clinically Oriented Review," *Clinical Psychology Review* 12 (1992): 93–116; D. C. Daley et al., "Increasing Treatment Compliance Among Outpatients with Comorbid Depression and Cocaine Dependence: Results of a Pilot Study," *American Journal of Psychiatry* (In Press); L. Simon-Onken, J. D. Blaine, and J. J. Boren, eds., "Beyond the Therapeutic Alliance: Keeping the Drug-Dependent Individual in Treatment," *National Institute on Drug Abuse Monograph 165* (Rockville, Md.: U.S. Department of Health and Human Services, 1997); D. D. Simpson, G. W. Joe, G. A. Rowan-Szal, and J. M. Greener, "Drug Abuse Treatment Process Components That Improve Retention," *Journal of Substance Abuse Treatment* 14, no. 6 (1997): 565–72; P. Gariti et al., "Effects of an Appointment Reminder Call on Patient Show Rates," *Journal of Substance Abuse Treatment* 12, no. 3 (1995): 207–12; J. D. Woody, "Clinical Strategies to Promote Compliance," *The American Journal of Family Therapy* 18, no. 3 (fall 1990): 285–94; R. M. Kadden and I. J. Mauriello, "Enhancing Participation in Substance Abuse Treatment Using an Incentive System," *Journal of Substance Abuse Treatment* 8 (1991): 113–24; W. M. Cox and E. Klinger, "A Motivational Model of Alcohol Use," *Journal of Abnormal Psychology* 97, no. 2 (1988): 168–80; W. Pfeiffer, W. Feuerlein, and E. Brenk-Schulte, "The Motivation of Alcohol Dependents to Undergo Treatment," *Drug and Alcohol Dependence* 29 (1991): 87–95; C. Anderson and S. Stewart, *Mastering Resistance* (New York: Guilford Press, 1983); P. Hayward et al., "Medication Self-Management: A Preliminary Report on an Intervention to Improve Medication Compliance," *Journal of Mental Health* 4 (1995): 511–17; R. Kemp, A. David, and P. Hayward, "Compliance Therapy: An Intervention Targeting Insight and Treatment Adherence in Psychotic Patients," *Behavioural and Cognitive Psychotherapy* 24 (1996): 331–50.
2. G. A. Marlatt, "Help-Seeking by Substance Abusers: The Role of Harm Reduction and Behavioral-Economic Approaches to Facilitate Treatment Entry and Retention," *in* L. Simon-Onken, J. D. Blaine, and J. J. Boren, eds., "Beyond the Therapeutic Alliance: Keeping the Drug-Dependent Individual in Treatment," *National Institute on Drug Abuse Monograph 165* (Rockville, Md.: U.S. Department of Health and Human Services, 1997): 44–84.
3. D. C. Daley and A. Zuckoff, "Improving Compliance with the Initial Outpatient Session Among Discharged Inpatient Dual Diagnosis Clients," *Social Work* 43, no. 5 (1998): 470–73.
4. D. C. Daley and M. E. Thase, *Dual Disorders Recovery Counseling: A Biopsychosocial Approach to Addiction and Mental Health Disorders* (Independence, Mo.: Herald House/Independence Press, 1994).
5. A. T. Beck et al., *Cognitive Therapy of Substance Abuse* (New York: Guilford Press,

1993); W. E. McAuliffe and J. Albert, *Clean Start: An Outpatient Program for Initiating Cocaine Recovery* (New York: Guilford Press, 1992); P. M. Monti et al., *Treating Alcohol Dependence* (New York: Guilford Press, 1989); D. C. Daley and G. A. Marlatt, *Managing Your Drug or Alcohol Problem Therapist Guide* (San Antonio: Psychological Corporation, 1997); D. C. Daley and G. A. Marlatt, *Managing Your Drug or Alcohol Problem Client Workbook* (San Antonio: Psychological Corporation, 1997); D. C. Daley, D. Mercer, and G. Carpenter, *Group Drug Counseling Manual* (Holmes Beach, Fla.: Learning Publications, 1998); National Institute on Alcohol Abuse and Alcoholism, "Cognitive-Behavioral Coping Skills Therapy Manual: A Clinical Research Guide for Therapists Treating Individuals with Alcohol Abuse and Dependence," *Project MATCH Monograph Series, Vol. 3* (Rockville, Md.: U.S. Department of Health and Human Services, 1995); National Institute on Alcohol Abuse and Alcoholism, "Motivational Enhancement Therapy Manual: A Clinical Research Guide for Therapists Treating Individuals with Alcohol Abuse and Dependence," *Project MATCH Monograph Series, Vol. 2* (Rockville, Md.: U.S. Department of Health and Human Services, 1995); National Institute on Alcohol Abuse and Alcoholism, "Twelve Step Facilitation Therapy Manual: A Clinical Research Guide for Therapists Treating Individuals with Alcohol Abuse and Dependence," *Project MATCH Monograph Series, Vol. 1* (Rockville, Md.: U.S. Department of Health and Human Services, 1995); National Institute on Drug Abuse, "A Community Reinforcement Plus Vouchers Approach: Treating Cocaine Addiction," *in* A. J. Budney and S. T. Higgins, *Therapy Manuals for Drug Addiction, Man. 2* (Rockville, Md.: U.S. Department of Health and Human Services, 1998); National Institute on Drug Abuse, "A Cognitive-Behavioral Approach: Treating Cocaine Addiction," *in* K. M. Carroll, *Therapy Manuals for Drug Addiction, Man. 1* (Rockville, Md.: U.S. Department of Health and Human Services, 1998).

6. M. D. Stanton, "The Role of Family and Significant Others in the Engagement and Retention of Drug-Dependent Individuals," *in* L. Simon-Onken, J. D. Blaine, and J. J. Boren, eds., "Beyond the Therapeutic Alliance: Keeping the Drug-Dependent Individual in Treatment," *National Institute on Drug Abuse Monograph 165* (Rockville, Md.: U.S. Department of Health and Human Services, 1997): 157–80; M. D. Stanton and A. W. Heath, "Family and Marital Therapy," *in* J. H. Lowinson et al., eds., *Substance Abuse: A Comprehensive Textbook*, 3d ed. (Baltimore: Williams & Wilkins, 1997): 448–54; J. Garrett et al., "ARISE: A Method for Engaging Reluctant Alcohol- and Drug-Dependent Individuals in Treatment," *Journal of Substance Abuse Treatment* (In Press).

7. *Patient Placement Criteria for the Treatment of Substance Related Disorders (ASAM PPC-2)*, 2d ed. (Chevy Chase, Md.: American Society of Addiction Medicine, 1996).

8. National Institute on Drug Abuse, "A Community Reinforcement Plus Vouchers

Approach"; S. T. Higgins et al., "Incentives Improve Outcome in Outpatient Behavioral Treatment of Cocaine Dependence," *Archives of General Psychiatry* 51 (1994): 568–76.

9. We administered the Davidson Social Phobia Questionnaire to 124 outpatients in our clinic. Over one-third reported significant symptoms of social anxiety and related avoidant behaviors.

10. A. T. Beck and G. Emergy, *Anxiety Disorders and Phobias: A Cognitive Perspective* (New York: Basic Books, 1985); L. Michelson and L. M. Ascher, eds., *Anxiety and Stress Disorders: Cognitive-Behavioral Assessment and Treatment* (New York: Guilford Press, 1987); R. E. Zinbarg, M. G. Craske, and D. H. Barlow, *Therapist's Guide for the Mastery of Your Anxiety and Worry* (Albany, N.Y.: Graywind Publications, 1993); M. G. Craske, D. H. Barlow, and T. O'Leary, *Mastery of Your Anxiety and Worry* (Albany, N.Y.: Graywind Publications, 1993); M. G. Craske, E. Meadows, and D.H. Barlow, *Therapist's Guide for the Mastery of Your Anxiety and Panic II & Agoraphobia Supplement* (Albany, N.Y.: Graywind Publications, 1994); D. H. Barlow and M. G. Craske, *Mastery of Your Anxiety and Panic II* (Albany, N.Y.: Graywind Publications, 1994).

11. Daley and Marlatt, *Managing Your Drug or Alcohol Problem Therapist Guide;* Daley and Marlatt, *Managing Your Drug or Alcohol Problem Client Workbook.*

12. D. C. Daley and G. A. Marlatt, "Relapse Prevention," *in* J. H. Lowinson et al., eds., *Substance Abuse: A Comprehensive Textbook,* 3d ed. (Baltimore: Williams & Wilkins, 1997): 458–66; D. C. Daley, *Relapse Prevention Workbook,* 2d ed. (Holmes Beach, Fla.: Learning Publications, 1997).

13. D. C. Daley, *Dual Diagnosis Workbook* (Independence, Mo.: Herald House/Independence Press, 1994).

14. R. P. Liberman, W. J. DeRisi, and K. T. Mueser, *Social Skills Training for Psychiatric Patients* (New York: Pergamon Press, 1989); R. P. Liberman et al., *Modules for Training Social and Independent Living Skills (Trainer's Manual, Patient's Workbook, Demonstration Video)* (Available from Psychiatric Rehabilitation Consultants, Camarillo-UCLA Research Center, Box A, Camarillo, Calif. 93011).

15. D. C. Daley and L. Roth, *When Symptoms Return: A Guide to Relapse in Psychiatric Illness* (Holmes Beach, Fla.: Learning Publications, 1992); D. C. Daley, *Preventing Relapse Workbook* (Center City, Minn.: Hazelden, 1993).

16. M. E. Thase and D. C. Daley, *Understanding Depression and Addiction Workbook* (Center City, Minn.: Hazelden, 1994); I. Salloum and D. C. Daley, *Understanding Anxiety Disorders and Addiction Workbook* (Center City, Minn.: Hazelden, 1994); R. Haskett and D. C. Daley, *Understanding Bipolar Disorder and Addiction Workbook* (Center City, Minn.: Hazelden, 1994); R. Weiss and D. C. Daley, *Understanding Personality Problems and Addiction Workbook* (Center City, Minn.: Hazelden, 1994); D. C. Daley and K. Montrose, *Understanding Schizophrenia and Addiction Workbook* (Center City, Minn.: Hazelden, 1994).

17. L. Simon-Onken, J. D. Blaine, and J. J. Boren, eds., "Integrating Behavioral Therapies with Medications in the Treatment of Drug Dependence," *National Institute on Drug Abuse Monograph 150* (Rockville, Md.: U.S. Department of Health and Human Services, 1995).
18. Daley and Marlatt, *Managing Your Drug or Alcohol Problem Therapist Guide.*
19. *The AA Member and Medications* (New York: Alcoholics Anonymous World Services, 1985).

Chapter 6
Systems and Agency Strategies to Improve Compliance

1. A. F. Lehman et al., "Prevalence and Patterns of 'Dual Diagnosis' Among Psychiatric Inpatients," *Comprehensive Psychiatry* 35, no. 2 (March/April 1994): 106–12; D. D. Simpson et al., "Drug Abuse Treatment Process Components That Improve Retention," *Journal of Substance Abuse Treatment* 14, no. 6 (1997): 565–72; R. M. Kadden and I. J. Mauriello, "Enhancing Participation in Substance Abuse Treatment Using an Incentive System," *Journal of Substance Abuse Treatment* 8 (1991): 113–24,133–34; D. Meichenbaum and D. C. Turk, *Facilitating Treatment Adherence: A Practitioner's Guidebook* (New York: Plenum Press, 1987); M. Matas, D. Staley, and W. Griffin, "A Profile of the Noncompliant Patient: A Thirty-Month Review of Outpatient Psychiatry Referrals," *General Hospital Psychiatry* 14 (1992): 124–30; M. J. Stark, B. K. Campbell, and C. V. Brinkerhoff, "Hello, May We Help You? A Study of Attrition Prevention at the Time of the First Phone Contact with Substance-Abusing Clients," *American Journal of Drug and Alcohol Abuse* 16, nos. 1 & 2 (1990): 67–76; J. A. Hoffman et al., "Comparative Cocaine Abuse Treatment Strategies: Enhancing Client Retention and Treatment Exposure," *Journal of Addictive Diseases* 13, no. 4 (1994): 115–28; N. J. Hochstadt and J. Trybula Jr., "Reducing Missed Initial Appointments in a Community Mental Health Center," *Journal of Community Psychology* 8 (1980): 261–65; W. M. Addenbrooke and N. H. Rathod, "Relationship Between Waiting Time and Retention in Treatment Amongst Substance Abusers," *Drug and Alcohol Dependence* 26 (1990): 255–64; B. Blackwell, ed., *Treatment Compliance and the Therapeutic Alliance* (Amsterdam: Harwood Academic Publishers, 1997).
2. National Institute on Alcohol Abuse and Alcoholism, "Motivational Enhancement Therapy Manual: A Clinical Research Guide for Therapists Treating Individuals with Alcohol Abuse and Dependence," *Project MATCH Monograph Series, Vol. 2* (Rockville, Md.: U.S. Department of Health and Human Services, 1995).
3. National Institute on Alcohol Abuse and Alcoholism, "Motivational Enhancement Therapy Manual"; W. R. Miller and S. Rollnick, *Motivational Interviewing: Preparing People to Change Addictive Behavior* (New York: Guilford Press, 1991); D. C. Daley et al., "Increasing Treatment Compliance Among Outpatients with Comorbid Depression and Cocaine Dependence: Results of a Pilot Study," *American Journal of Psychiatry* (In Press); R. Kemp et al., "Randomised Controlled

Trial of Compliance Therapy," *British Journal of Psychiatry* 172 (1998): 413–19; A. Healeyk et al., "Cost-Effective Evaluation of Compliance Therapy for People with Psychosis," *British Journal of Psychiatry* 172 (1998): 420–24.

4. D. S. Festinger et al., "Pretreatment Dropout as a Function of Treatment Delay and Client Variables," *Addictive Behaviors* 20, no. 1 (1995): 111–15.
5. J. O. Prochaska, J. C. Norcross, and C. C. DiClemente, *Changing for Good: The Revolutionary Program That Explains the Six Stages of Change and Teaches You How to Free Yourself from Bad Habits* (New York: William Morrow, 1994).
6. National Institute on Drug Abuse, "Progress and Issues in Case Management," *Research Monograph Series, Vol. 127* (Rockville, Md.: U.S. Department of Health and Human Services, 1992).
7. P. J. Bokos et al., "Case Management: An Alternative Approach to Working with Intravenous Drug Users," *Research Monograph Series, Vol. 127* (Rockville, Md.: U.S. Department of Health and Human Services, 1992): 92–111.
8. K. Minkoff, "Program Components of a Comprehensive Integrated Care System for Serious Mentally Ill Patients with Substance Disorders," *Dual Diagnosis of Major Mental Illness and Substance Disorder* (San Francisco: Jossey-Bass, 1991): 13–27.
9. K. Montrose and D. C. Daley, *Celebrating Small Victories: A Primer of Approaches and Attitudes for Helping Clients with Dual Disorders* (Center City, Minn.: Hazelden, 1995); Minkoff, "Program Components of a Comprehensive Integrated Care System for Serious Mentally Ill Patients with Substance Disorders," 13–27; D. C. Daley and M. E. Thase, *Dual Disorders Recovery Counseling: A Biopsychosocial Approach to Addiction and Mental Health Disorders* (Independence, Mo.: Herald House/Independence Press, 1994).
10. R. E. Drake et al., "The Course, Treatment and Outcome of Substance Disorder in Persons with Severe Mental Illness," *American Journal of Orthopsychiatry* 66, no. 1 (1996): 42-51; C. R. Miner et al., "Prediction of Compliance with Outpatient Referral in Patients with Schizophrenia and Psychoactive Substance Use Disorders," *Archives of General Psychiatry* 54 (1997): 706–12.

Chapter 7
A Motivational Approach to Improving Compliance

1. *Mickey's Favorites Sing-Along* (Burbank, Calif.: Walt Disney Records, 1995).
2. Project MATCH Research Group, "Matching Alcoholism Treatments to Client Heterogeneity: Project MATCH Posttreatment Outcomes," *Journal of Studies on Alcohol* 58 (1997): 7–29; W. R. Miller, "Increasing Motivation for Change," and W. R. Miller et al., "What Works? A Methodological Analysis of the Alcohol Treatment Outcome Literature," *in* R. K. Hester and W. R. Miller, eds., *Handbook of Alcoholism Treatment Approaches: Effective Alternatives*, 2d ed. (Needham Heights, Mass.: Allyn and Bacon, 1995); B. Saunders, C. Wilkinson, and M. Phillips, "The Impact of a Brief Motivational Intervention with Opiate Users Attending a Methadone Programme," *Addiction* 90 (1995): 415–24; W. R. Miller, R. G.

Benefield, and J. S. Tonigan, "Enhancing Motivation for Change in Problem Drinking: A Controlled Comparison of Two Therapist Styles," *Journal of Consulting and Clinical Psychology* 61 (1993): 455–61; T. H. Bien, W. R. Miller, and J. M. Boroughs, "Motivational Interviewing with Alcohol Outpatients," *Behavioural and Cognitive Psychotherapy* 21 (1993): 347-56.

3. D. C. Daley and M. E. Thase, *Dual Disorders Recovery Counseling: A Biopsychosocial Approach to Addiction and Mental Health Disorders* (Independence, Mo.: Herald House/Independence Press, 1994).

4. W. R. Miller, "Motivational Interviewing with Problem Drinkers," *Behavioural Psychotherapy* 11 (1983): 147–72; J. O. Prochaska, J. C. Norcross, and C. C. DiClemente, *Changing for Good: The Revolutionary Program That Explains the Six Stages of Change and Teaches You How to Free Yourself from Bad Habits* (New York: William Morrow, 1994); J. O. Prochaska, C. C. DiClemente, and J. C. Norcross, "In Search of How People Change: Applications to Addictive Behaviors," *American Psychologist* 47 (1992): 1102–14; J. O. Prochaska and C. C. DiClemente, "Transtheoretical Therapy: Toward a More Integrative Model of Change," *Psychotherapy: Theory, Research, and Practice* 19 (1982): 276–88.

5. A. Bandura, "Self-efficacy Mechanism in Human Agency," *American Psychologist* 37 (1982): 122–47.

6. E. Erikson, *Childhood and Society*, 2d ed. (New York: W. W. Norton, 1963), 247.

7. D. Mark and J. Faude, *Psychotherapy of Cocaine Addiction: Entering the Interpersonal World of the Cocaine Addict* (Livingston, N.J.: Jason Aronson, 1997), 163.

Chapter 8
Pretreatment Motivational Counseling

1. W. R. Miller et al., "What Works? A Methodological Analysis of the Alcohol Treatment Outcome Literature," *in* R. K. Hester and W. R. Miller, eds. *Handbook of Alcoholism Treatment Approaches: Effective Alternatives*, 2d ed. (Needham Heights, Mass.: Allyn and Bacon, 1995). Miller and his associates continue to update their meta-analysis of alcohol treatment effectiveness; the version dated April 1997, presented at the eighth International Conference on the Treatment of Addictive Behaviors in Sante Fe, New Mexico (January 1998), has not been published at the time of this writing but continues to show the same overall results.

2. T. H. Bien, W. R. Miller, and J. S. Tonigan, "Brief Interventions for Alcohol Problems: A Review," *Addiction* 88 (1993): 315–36.

3. W. R. Miller and S. Rollnick, *Motivational Interviewing: Preparing People to Change Addictive Behavior* (New York: Guilford Press, 1991), 32–34.

4. See, for example, National Institute on Alcohol Abuse and Alcoholism, "Motivational Enhancement Therapy Manual: A Clinical Research Guide for Therapists Treating Individuals with Alcohol Abuse and Dependence," *Project*

MATCH Monograph Series, Vol. 2 (Rockville, Md.: U.S. Department of Health and Human Services, 1995).

5. Miller and Rollnick, *Motivational Interviewing*, 80–83.
6. Ibid., 56–58.
7. Miller et al., "What Works?"
8. G. Woody et al., "Psychotherapy for Opiate Addicts: Does It Help?" *Archives of General Psychiatry* 40 (1983): 639–45.
9. B. Saunders, C. Wilkinson, and M. Phillips, "The Impact of a Brief Motivational Intervention with Opiate Users Attending a Methadone Programme," *Addiction* 90 (1995): 415–24.
10. See, for example, D. Mark and J. Faude, *Psychotherapy of Cocaine Addiction: Entering the Interpersonal World of the Cocaine Addict* (Livingston, N.J.: Jason Aronson, 1997); J. A. Hoffman et al., "Comparative Cocaine Abuse Treatment Strategies: Enhancing Client Retention and Treatment Exposure," *Experimental Therapeutics in Addiction Medicine* 13, no. 4 (1994).
11. See, for example, D. C. Daley and M. E. Thase, *Dual Disorders Recovery Counseling: A Biopsychosocial Approach to Addiction and Mental Health Disorders* (Independence, Mo.: Herald House/Independence Press, 1994).
12. J. Trimpey, *The Small Book: A Revolutionary Alternative for Overcoming Alcohol and Drug Dependence* (New York: Delacorte Press, 1992).
13. A. Kishline, *Moderate Drinking: The New Option for Problem Drinkers* (Tucson, Ariz.: See Sharp Press, 1994).
14. C. Rogers, *Client-Centered Therapy* (Boston: Houghton, 1951).
15. R. Schafer, *The Analytic Attitude* (New York: Basic Books, 1983).
16. C. Rogers, "The Necessary and Sufficient Conditions of Therapeutic Personality Change," *Journal of Consulting Psychology* 21 (1957): 95–103.
17. A. Bandura, "Self-efficacy Mechanism in Human Agency," *American Psychologist* 37 (1982): 122–47.
18. See, for example, M. L. Seltzer, "The Michigan Alcoholism Screening Test: The Quest for a New Diagnostic Instrument," *American Journal of Psychiatry* 127 (1971): 1653–58; H. A. Skinner, "The Drug Abuse Screening Test," *Addictive Behavior* 7 (1982): 363–71.
19. American Psychiatric Association, *Diagnostic and Statistical Manual of Mental Disorders*, 4th ed. (Washington, D.C.: American Psychiatric Association, 1994).
20. Miller and Rollnick refer to this as "double-sided reflection"; see *Motivational Interviewing*, 105.

Chapter 9
Transitional Motivational Counseling

1. J. M. Brown and W. R. Miller, "Impact of Motivational Interviewing on Participation and Outcome in Residential Alcoholism Treatment," *Psychology of Addictive Behaviors* 7 (1993): 211–18, and L. L. Aubrey, "Motivational

Interviewing with Adolescents Presenting for Outpatient Substance Abuse Treatment" (Ph.D. diss., University of New Mexico, 1998), for accounts of interventions developed for a similar purpose.

2. D. C. Daley, "A Psychoeducational Approach to Relapse Prevention," *Journal of Chemical Dependency Treatment* 2 (1989): 105–24; D.C. Daley, "Relapse Prevention with Substance Abusers: Clinical Issues and Myths," *Social Work* 32 (1987): 138–42; D. C. Daley and M. E. Thase, *Dual Disorders Recovery Counseling: A Biopsychosocial Approach to Addiction and Mental Health Disorders* (Independence, Mo.: Herald House/Independence Press, 1994).
3. L. Wurmser, "The Role of Superego Conflicts in Substance Abuse and Their Treatment," *International Journal of Psychoanalytic Psychotherapy* 10 (1984–85): 227–58.
4. C. Dunn, "Motivational Interviewing: When Less Is More" (lecture given at the University of Pittsburgh Medical Center, Pittsburgh, Pa., June 1997). See C. Dunn, "Motivation to Change," *Professional Counselor* (June 1996): 41–45 for a description of his application of motivational principles to improving treatment compliance.

Chapter 10
Motivational Counseling in Early Recovery

1. L. E. Beutler, H. Zetzer, and E. Yost, "Tailoring Interventions to Clients: Effects on Engagement and Retention," *in* L. Simon-Onken, J. D. Blaine, and J. J. Boren, eds., "Beyond the Therapeutic Alliance: Keeping the Drug-Dependent Individual in Treatment," *National Institute on Drug Abuse Monograph 165* (Rockville, Md.: U.S. Department of Health and Human Services, 1997): 85–109.
2. See C. C. DiClemente and C. W. Scott, "Stages of Change: Interactions with Treatment Compliance and Involvement," *in* L. Simon-Onken, J. D. Blaine, and J. J. Boren, eds. "Beyond the Therapeutic Alliance: Keeping the Drug-Dependent Individual in Treatment," *National Institute on Drug Abuse Monograph 165* (Rockville, Md.: U.S. Department of Health and Human Services, 1997): 131–56; also J. M. Somers and G. A. Marlatt, "Alcohol Problems," *in* P. H. Wilson, ed., *Principles and Practice of Relapse Prevention* (New York: Guilford Press, 1992).
3. S. Rollnick and W .R. Miller, "What Is Motivational Interviewing?" *Behavioural and Cognitive Psychotherapy* 23 (1995): 325–34.
4. J. O. Prochaska, J. C. Norcross, and C. C. DiClemente, *Changing for Good: The Revolutionary Program That Explains the Six Stages of Change and Teaches You How to Free Yourself from Bad Habits* (New York: William Morrow, 1994).
5. See, for example, D. C. Daley and G. A. Marlatt, *Managing Your Drug or Alcohol Problem Therapist Guide* (San Antonio: Psychological Corporation, 1997); D. C. Daley and G. A. Marlatt, *Managing Your Drug or Alcohol Problem Client Workbook* (San Antonio: Psychological Corporation, 1997); National Institute on Alcohol Abuse and Alcoholism, "Cognitive-Behavioral Coping Skills Therapy

Manual: A Clinical Research Guide for Therapists Treating Individuals with Alcohol Abuse and Dependence," *Project MATCH Monograph Series, Vol. 3* (Rockville, Md.: U.S. Department of Health and Human Services, 1995).

6. W. R. Miller and S. Rollnick, *Motivational Interviewing: Preparing People to Change Addictive Behavior* (New York: Guilford Press, 1991), 58–60.
7. W. R. Miller and A. Page, "Warm Turkey: Alternative Routes to Abstinence," *Journal of Substance Abuse Treatment* 8 (1991): 227–32.
8. See, for example, A. Kishline, *Moderate Drinking: The New Option for Problem Drinkers* (Tuscon, Ariz.: See Sharp Press, 1994), 90–94.
9. Miller and Rollnick, *Motivational Interviewing,* 119–21.
10. D. Mark and L. Luborsky, *A Manual for the Use of Supportive-Expressive Psychotherapy in the Treatment of Cocaine Abuse* (Department of Psychiatry, Hospital of the University of Pennsylvania: unpublished, 1992).
11. L. Luborsky et al., "The Efficacy of Dynamic Psychotherapies: Is It True That 'Everyone Has Won and All Must Have Prizes'?" *in* N. E. Miller et al., eds., *Psychodynamic Treatment Research: A Handbook for Clinical Practice* (New York: Basic Books, 1993): 497–516; L. Luborsky et al., "Therapist Success and Its Determinants," *Archives of General Psychiatry* 42 (1985): 605–11; S. K. Valle, "Interpersonal Functioning of Alcoholism Counselors and Treatment Outcome," *Journal of Studies on Alcohol* 42 (1981): 783–90. Note that despite heroic efforts to differentiate the effectiveness of treatments for alcohol abuse for different clients, the researchers of Project MATCH found that all three tested treatments were quite effective overall without being able robustly to match treatment to personality factor; Project MATCH Research Group, "Matching Alcoholism Treatments to Client Heterogeneity: Project MATCH Posttreatment Outcomes," *Journal of Studies on Alcohol* 58 (1997): 7–29.
12. See National Institute on Alcohol Abuse and Alcoholism, "Motivational Enhancement Therapy Manual: A Clinical Research Guide for Therapists Treating Individuals with Alcohol Abuse and Dependence," *Project MATCH Monograph Series, Vol. 2* (Rockville, Md.: U. S. Department of Health and Human Services, 1995), for a list of psychosocial, physiological, and neurological assessment tools; see also L. Derogatis, R. Lipman, and K. Rickels, "The Hopkins Symptom Checklist (HSCL: A Self-Report Symptom Inventory)," *Behavioral Science* 19 (1974): 1–16; M. Hamilton, "A Psychiatric Rating Scale for Depression," *Journal of Neurological and Neurosurgical Psychiatry* 23 (1960): 56–62; A. T. McClellan et al., "An Improved Evaluation Instrument for Alcohol and Drug Use Patients," *Journal of Nervous and Mental Disorders* 163 (1980): 26–33 (the "Addiction Severity Index"); R. D. Weiss, M. L. Griffin, S. M. Mirin, "Diagnosing Major Depression in Cocaine Abusers: The Use of Depression Rating Scales," *PsychiatryRes* 28 (1989): 335–43.
13. See National Institute on Alcohol Abuse and Alcoholism, "Motivational Enhancement Therapy Manual," 89–90, for an example of a feedback form.

14. Miller and Rollnick, *Motivational Interveuing*, 96–99.
15. C. T. Fischer, *Individualizing Psychological Assessment* (Monterey, Calif.: Brooks/Cole, 1985).
16. Miller and Rollnick, *Motivational Interviewing*, 104.
17. G. A. Marlatt and J. R. Gordon, eds., *Relapse Prevention: Maintenance Strategies in the Treatment of Addictive Disorders* (New York: Guilford Press, 1985), 41–43.
18. Daley and Marlatt, *Managing Your Drug or Alcohol Problem Therapist Guide;* Daley and Marlatt, *Managing Your Drug or Alcohol Problem Client Workbook.*
19. See S. Shiffman et al., "Preventing Relapse in Ex-Smokers: A Self-Management Approach," *in* G. A. Marlatt and J. R. Gordon, eds., *Relapse Prevention*, 472–520, for an extended example of relapse debriefing in a group context.
20. Miller and Rollnick, *Motivational Interviewing*, 117.

Index

Page numbers for charts are set in italics.

About the Authors

Dennis C. Daley, Ph. D. is director of the Center for Psychiatric and Chemical Dependency Services and an associate professor of psychiatry at the University of Pittsburgh Medical Center, Department of Psychiatry, at Western Psychiatric Institute and Clinic in Pittsburgh. Daley has been involved in managing and providing treatment services for people with alcohol and other drug problems and dual disorders for over two decades. He has written over 125 publications including journal articles, books, clinical manuals, client workbooks, and recovery guides. Daley has authored numerous Hazelden publications including *Dual Disorders: Counseling Clients with Chemical Dependency and Mental Illness; Celebrating Small Victories; A Family Guide to Dual Disorders; Coping with Dual Disorders; Preventing Relapse* (workbook); *Understanding Major Anxiety Disorders and Addiction* (workbook); *Understanding Bipolar Disorder and Addiction* (workbook); *Understanding Depression and Addiction* (workbook); *Understanding Personality Problems and Addiction* (workbook); and *Understanding Schizophrenia and Addiction* (pamphlet and workbook). He teaches on these subjects throughout the United States and other countries. Daley is also involved in several federally funded research projects on treatment of cocaine addiction and treatment of dual disorders. Daley authored the highly successful Living Sober I and Living Sober II Interactive Videotape Series and the Promise of Recovery Educational Videotape Series.

Allan Zuckoff, M.A., is a clinical supervisor and codirector of training at the Center for Psychiatric and Chemical Dependency Services, Western Psychiatric Institute and Clinic, University of Pittsburgh Medical Center. He is a trainer in Motivational Interviewing and is currently directing the training and supervision of therapists for federally funded studies of the application of the motivational approach to substance dependence and depression and to HIV risk-reduction. He has also been a supportive-expressive psychotherapist for a multisite study of psychosocial treatments for cocaine addiction. Zuckoff has led workshops on a range of topics related to substance abuse and dual-disorders treatment, and he provides consultation on motivational interventions to a number of agencies. He is a doctoral candidate in clinical psychology at Duquesne University and an adjunct instructor at Seton Hill College in Greensburg, Pennsylvania.

HAZELDEN INFORMATION AND EDUCATIONAL SERVICES is a division of the Hazelden Foundation, a not-for-profit organization. Since 1949, Hazelden has been a leader in promoting the dignity and treatment of people afflicted with the disease of chemical dependency.

The mission of the foundation is to improve the quality of life for individuals, families, and communities by providing a national continuum of information, education, and recovery services that are widely accessible; to advance the field through research and training; and to improve our quality and effectiveness through continuous improvement and innovation.

Stemming from that, the mission of this division is to provide quality information and support to people wherever they may be in their personal journey—from education and early intervention, through treatment and recovery, to personal and spiritual growth.

Although our treatment programs do not necessarily use everything Hazelden publishes, our bibliotherapeutic materials support our mission and the Twelve Step philosophy upon which it is based. We encourage your comments and feedback.

The headquarters of the Hazelden Foundation is in Center City, Minnesota. Additional treatment facilities are located in Chicago, Illinois; New York, New York; Plymouth, Minnesota; St. Paul, Minnesota; and West Palm Beach, Florida. At these sites, we provide a continuum of care for men and women of all ages. Our Plymouth facility is designed specifically for youth and families.

For more information on Hazelden, please call **1-800-257-7800.** Or you may access our World Wide Web site on the Internet at **www.hazelden.org.**